SpringerBriefs in Finance

SpringerBriefs present concise summaries of cutting-edge research and practical applications across a wide spectrum of fields. Featuring compact volumes of 50 to 125 pages, the series covers a range of content from professional to academic. Typical topics might include: a timely report of state-of-the art analytical techniques, a bridge between new research results, as published in journal articles, and a contextual literature review, a snapshot of a hot or emerging topic, an in-depth case study or clinical example, and a presentation of core concepts that students must understand in order to make independent contributions. SpringerBriefs in Finance showcase emerging theory, empirical research, and practical application in corporate finance, banking, financial management, behavioral finance, financial markets, social and entrepreneurial finance, microfinance, and related fields, from a global author community. Briefs are characterized by fast, global electronic dissemination, standard publishing contracts, standardized manuscript preparation and formatting guidelines, and expedited production schedules.

Davide Sandretto

Cryptocurrencies as an Asset Class

An Overview

Springer

Davide Sandretto
University of Turin
Turin, Italy

ISSN 2193-1720 ISSN 2193-1739 (electronic)
SpringerBriefs in Finance
ISBN 978-3-032-31490-1 ISBN 978-3-032-31491-8 (eBook)
https://doi.org/10.1007/978-3-032-31491-8

This Springer imprint is published by the registered company Springer Nature Switzerland AG
The registered company address is: Gewerbestrasse 11, 6330 Cham, Switzerland

This book is dedicated to my family.

Introduction

Although cryptocurrencies are no longer a new phenomenon, as nearly two decades have passed since the creation of Bitcoin, this subject remains poorly understood and underexplored. Cryptocurrencies sit at the intersection of computer science and economics, a position that demands a thorough and rigorous study of the topic in order to fully understand the value and potential opportunities that this emerging asset class represents.

Today, cryptocurrencies constitute a market that can no longer be ignored, with a total market capitalization of approximately 3 trillion US dollars as of the end of December 2025. This scale makes them an increasingly attractive asset class, one with the potential to enhance an investor's portfolio by improving its efficiency through the lens of the mean-variance framework. A deeper understanding of the phenomenon, of how cryptocurrencies function and how they differ from one another at a structural level, is therefore essential for any investor seeking to make informed and sound decisions. Equally, a stronger knowledge base serves as a powerful tool for identifying which projects are genuinely worthy of investment and which, conversely, represent little more than marketing traps that exploit hype to fuel speculative bubbles.

This book approaches cryptocurrencies first from a technical standpoint, then from a financial one. More specifically, the first chapter traces the history of the creation of Bitcoin, analyzing its underlying mechanics and its technical aspects. The chapter then covers the evolution of blockchain technology, focusing in particular on the introduction of smart contracts, and examines Ethereum as another major player in the market, together with the broader ecosystem it has given rise to, from tokens to decentralized applications. This chapter will be of particular interest to readers who wish to develop a thorough understanding of how a blockchain operates and how its native currency functions within it.

The second chapter proposes a taxonomy and classification of cryptocurrencies based on their operational design and underlying infrastructure. It will be especially valuable to those seeking a clear and structured overview of the cryptocurrency ecosystem, as understanding the different typologies is a crucial prerequisite for any informed investor.

The third chapter conducts a systematic literature review on the role of cryptocurrencies as a financial asset. Drawing on academic research from the earliest published articles to the present, it employs a quantitative approach through bibliometric analysis. Readers will gain a comprehensive view of the state of the art in this field and become acquainted with the most influential studies examining cryptocurrencies as a new asset class and their relationship with more traditional asset classes.

The fourth and final chapter closes the book with an empirical analysis addressing the central question of whether cryptocurrencies can represent a meaningful diversification opportunity for investors pursuing an efficient portfolio strategy. In particular, it separately and jointly analyzes the performance of various asset classes, including equities, bonds, commodities, and cryptocurrencies, applying a mean-variance optimization framework.

Overall, this book is intended for individuals who wish to understand cryptocurrencies both from a financial perspective and at a deeper technical level, grasping how they function, what their potential may be, and how to navigate the heterogeneity that characterizes this asset class.

Competing Interests The author has no competing interests to declare that are relevant to the content of this manuscript.

Contents

Chapter 1
Blockchain Technology and Cryptocurrencies

1.1 The Origin of Bitcoin

Bitcoin was the first cryptocurrency created by an unknown person or group of people under the pseudonym of Satoshi Nakamoto. On the 31st of October 2008, the whitepaper explaining the idea of Bitcoin was made public (Nakamoto, 2008), and some time later the open source Bitcoin software, now known as Bitcoin Core, was released. This software runs the Bitcoin system and could, in principle, be downloaded on a wide range of computing devices, including laptops and smartphones, making the technology easily accessible to anyone. In practice, however, given the considerable growth in the size of the data stored on the blockchain over the years, running the complete version of the software today requires a computer with substantial storage capacity and computational power.

The idea of Satoshi Nakamoto was revolutionary. It entailed the construction of a peer to peer decentralized transaction system via the Internet, allowing individuals to transfer money to each other without the need for any intermediary, such as banks. Its timing was far from coincidental, as the Bitcoin whitepaper was published at the height of the global financial crisis, a period marked by widespread distrust towards a financial system dominated by centralized institutions. The symbolic act marking Bitcoin's creation in opposition to traditional finance is still visible today.[1] The text inscribed in the genesis block, which is the first block of transactions recorded on the Bitcoin blockchain, states: "The Times 03/Jan/2009 Chancellor on brink of second bailout for banks". The message, illustrated in Fig. 1.1, reproduces the front page headline of the British newspaper The Times on the third of January 2009, reporting on the imminent bailout by the British

[1] Visiting this address on the blockchain explorer blockchain.com https://www.blockchain.com/explorer/blocks/btc/0, it is possible to observe the details of the first block of the Bitcoin blockchain, known as the genesis block, as well as the text inscribed by Nakamoto himself.

D. Sandretto, *Cryptocurrencies as an Asset Class*, SpringerBriefs in Finance,
https://doi.org/10.1007/978-3-032-31491-8_1

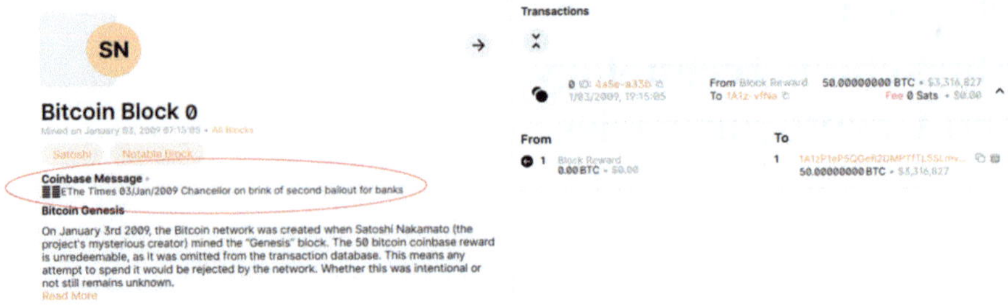

Fig. 1.1 Bitcoin genesis block. Source: Blockchain.com

Government of struggling banks during the financial crisis. Within the community, this inscription has been widely interpreted as a deliberate statement of intent, embedding in the very foundation of Bitcoin a critique of centralized monetary systems and the institutions that govern them.

Beyond its symbolic significance, the technical architecture conceived by Nakamoto represents a radical departure from the traditional system, indeed. In conventional transactions, an intermediary serves as a trusted third party responsible for verifying that the sender holds sufficient funds, ensuring those funds are not spent more than once (a problem known as double-spending), and recording the transaction in a private, centralized ledger. In contrast, the system envisioned in Nakamoto's whitepaper sought to replace this figure with a decentralized network that, through a set of rules and incentives, could provide the same guarantees. But how can this be possible?

Nakamoto's answer to this challenge was to eliminate the need to trust any single party altogether by making the entire system transparent and collectively verifiable. To achieve this, the idea was to rely on Distributed Ledger Technology (DLT), namely a public, distributed transaction ledger accessible to everyone, so that anyone could transparently observe the transactions recorded on it. This also eliminates the single-point-of-failure problem, where a bug could cause the entire system to shut down.

The distributed ledger is built from a series of transactions, collected into data blocks that are progressively appended to form a chain. This is why it is called Blockchain. Transactions are managed and validated by the network's nodes, that is, all computers running the Bitcoin software and holding a copy of the ledger. Because anyone can download the software and join the network freely, Bitcoin is classified as a permissionless or public blockchain, in contrast to permissioned or private blockchains, where participation requires verified and authorized identities.

Transactions on the Bitcoin blockchain are not denominated in fiat currency but in bitcoin,[2] the network's native currency. This currency does not exist physically and is implied within the transactions carried out between parties. It is created every

[2] Bitcoin is written with a lowercase "b" when referring to the digital currency, and with an uppercase "B" when referring to the network and protocol.

time a block of transactions is processed by nodes, which in this context are called miners, and awarded to them as a reward for the work performed. The first bitcoins were therefore created through the generation of blocks by miners and subsequently exchanged and distributed across the network. As of December 2025, the total amount of circulating bitcoin is almost 20 million, with the maximum foreseen supply set arbitrarily at 21 million, a figure that will be reached mathematically around the year 2141.

Further to eliminating the need for a central intermediary, Bitcoin was also conceived as a direct improvement over the existing payment infrastructure, promising faster and more secure transactions at a lower cost.

In the traditional system, at least in the European context, transactions undergo a clearing process in which multilateral positions between banks are netted following a verification of the correctness and regularity of the operation. The resulting net position is then settled through the TARGET2 system, today evolved into the T2 system, governed by the European Central Bank and the central banks of the union. This process introduces an inherent delay in the final receipt of funds by the beneficiary, who will normally have access to them at t + 2.[3] In the context of international cross-border transactions, timeframes could be even longer, as the clearing and settlement process follows the correspondent banking system.

Bitcoin addressed these limitations on multiple fronts. It imposed no cross-border restrictions, allowing anyone anywhere in the world to transact within the same timeframes as a domestic payment. Unlike traditional systems, which operate on business days and are subject to periods of inactivity due to holidays, Bitcoin operates autonomously 24 hours a day, 7 days a week. With regard to fees, costs are not tied to the amount transacted but are instead proportional to the space the transaction occupies in the block, which depends on the number of inputs and outputs it contains, resulting in a markedly more efficient fee structure. Consistently, several studies in the literature demonstrate that the Bitcoin network holds significant advantages in terms of fees compared to traditional channels (Chiu & Koeppl, 2017; Lehar & Parlour, 2019; Sajter, 2022). As a striking illustration of this, Fig. 1.2 depicts block number 903,916 mined on the fourth of July 2025, in which around 10,000 bitcoins were moved across different addresses, transferring over 1 billion US dollars in value while incurring a fee of just 40.46 US dollars.

Bitcoin thus emerged in 2008 as a new instrument for transactions, competing with the traditional financial system. Over the years, however, new applications and new cryptocurrencies have been developed. The next sections describe in detail how the blockchain, transactions, and the structure of the Bitcoin network work, while also illustrating the developments this new technology has undergone.

[3] This was the standard functioning of payment systems at the time of Bitcoin's inception. Today, infrastructures such as TARGET Instant Payment Settlement (TIPS) allow transactions to be carried out 24/7 in real time every day of the year.

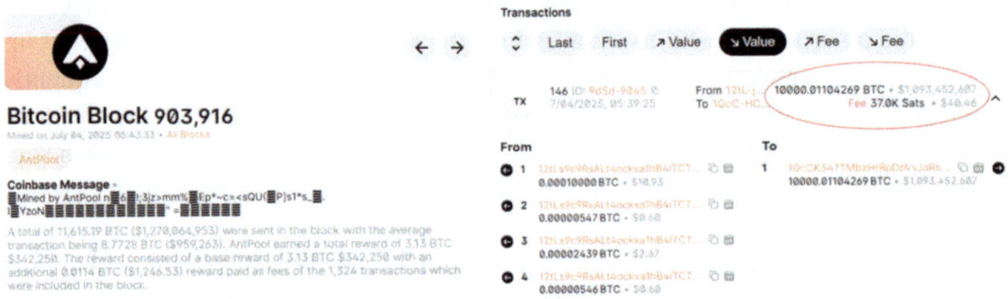

Fig. 1.2 Bitcoin block number 903,916. Source: Blockchain.com

1.2 Keys and Wallet

The Bitcoin network relies on a cryptographic system of keys to verify ownership and authorize transactions. Let us assume that two individuals, Alice and Bob, want to exchange 1 bitcoin. Specifically, Alice holds 1 bitcoin from a previous transaction and wants to send it to Bob. In order to make such a transaction and prove she actually has 1 bitcoin, Alice needs a private key and a public key.

The private key is a randomly generated string of 256 binary digits (expressed as 64 hexadecimal characters), producing an astronomically large number of possible combinations that makes it virtually impossible to guess. It must never be shared, as whoever holds it effectively controls the bitcoins associated with the corresponding address. Indeed, through the private key, it is possible to digitally sign transactions, that is, to provide mathematical proof that one knows the private key. In the context of our example, if someone were to obtain Alice's private key, her funds could be stolen and transferred elsewhere without her consent. Equally important is not losing the private key, as Alice would no longer have access to her funds and there is no way to recover them, since no central authority exists that could restore access on her behalf.

The public key, on the other hand, is derived from the private one through a mathematical process called elliptic curve multiplication. The generated key is no longer a random number but is instead represented by the coordinates of a point on the elliptic curve (x and y), from which it is not possible to derive the private key, as the calculation is one-way only and therefore not reversible.[4] Only through brute force one could attempt to do so. However, given its very large size, this is practically impossible using the technologies currently available.

The public key is shared openly and forms part of the transaction inputs, allowing the network to verify that whoever executed the transaction had the right to do so. This is done by checking that the digital signature is correct and therefore that the party who made the transaction is the holder of the private key, without this ever being revealed. In other words, the network can confirm that Alice is the legitimate

[4]For further details on elliptic curve cryptography and the construction and formats of keys, the reader is referred to Antonopoulos (2017).

owner of the funds she is sending to Bob, without Alice ever disclosing her private key. This mechanism is fundamental to the functioning of a decentralized system, as asymmetric cryptography allows the ownership of funds to be verified easily and transparently, without the need for any third party.

From the public key, it is possible to derive the Bitcoin address through one-way cryptographic hashing. The address is a string of numbers and letters ranging from 26 to 35 characters, depending on the format, and represents the reference point for sending and receiving funds, much like a bank account number. Bob, for instance, shares his Bitcoin address with Alice so that she can direct the funds to him. Although an address can be reused, the common practice is to generate a new one for each transaction, along with the corresponding keys, to improve privacy by making it harder to trace a user's balance and to enhance overall security.

The private and public keys described above are normally created and stored in a wallet, a software application that serves as a user interface through which individuals can manage and sign transactions, handle keys and addresses, and check their cryptocurrency balance. It is important to note that the wallet does not store bitcoins themselves, but only the corresponding keys. The bitcoins exist exclusively on the blockchain, and the wallet simply reads the transactions recorded there to calculate and display the available balance.

There are different types of wallets. A first broad distinction is between hot wallets and cold wallets:

- Hot wallets: wallets that store private and public keys while maintaining a connection to the Internet. The management of transactions is faster, making them a preferable solution for those who frequently need to make payments. However, being constantly connected to the Internet, hot wallets are more exposed to cyberattacks and therefore considered less secure than their offline counterparts.
- Cold wallets: wallets that store private and public keys offline. The management of transactions is slower, as they are prepared on an Internet-connected device and the cold wallet is then used to apply the digital signature offline. Once this is done, the signed transactions are uploaded back onto the Internet-connected device and broadcasted to the blockchain. Since the keys never leave the offline environment of the cold wallet, the risk of theft is minimal, making this the safest option for storing keys.

In relation to the interface used to access wallet services, hot wallets can be divided into 3 categories:

- Desktop wallet: a software application that can be downloaded on a computer, granting full control over one's keys, as they are stored locally on the hard disk, and giving a high degree of autonomy in managing transactions. It was the original reference implementation of wallets. Even though keys are stored locally, the risk of hacking remains, as an Internet connection exposes the device to cyberattacks. An example of a desktop wallet for making Bitcoin transactions is Electrum.

- Web wallet: a wallet that can be accessed via a web browser, allowing quick access without requiring wallet software to be installed on the computer. However, the wallet runs on a third-party server. Some web wallets, such as Unisat Wallet, allow users to retain full control of their keys, while others, such as those operated by crypto exchanges like Binance and Coinbase, hold the keys on behalf of the user in exchange for a simpler and more accessible experience.
- Mobile wallet: an application downloaded on the smartphone designed for an easy user experience. Similar to web wallets, the third-party provider can either have access to your keys (e.g. Coinbase app) or not (e.g. Exodus).

Cold wallets, on the other hand, are distinguished into:

- Hardware wallet: a device that hosts a secure wallet and stores the keys offline. It is used to sign transactions by connecting the physical hardware via USB for desktop or web wallets, or via NFC (Near-field communication) for mobile wallets. Popular examples include devices from Trezor and Ledger, which resemble a USB drive in size and form. This is widely regarded as the most secure option for storing keys.
- Paper wallet: a physical document on which the private key is printed, sometimes accompanied by the public key. Being entirely offline, it is inherently secure from cyberattacks. However, due to its inflexibility it has largely fallen out of use, superseded by hardware wallets.

If someone owns a large amount of bitcoin and intends to hold it over the long term, it is advisable to store the private keys in a cold wallet such as a hardware wallet, in order to minimize the risk of theft. If instead one holds only a small amount and makes payments frequently, a hot wallet would be the more practical choice.

Based on who has ownership of the private keys, wallets can also be divided into:

- Custodial wallets: the user entrusts a third party with custody of the keys, meaning that the third party manages and secures them. This type of wallet is characteristic of crypto exchanges, which handle the technical aspects on the user's behalf and enable less experienced users to manage cryptocurrency transactions more easily. In the event of lost credentials (those used to access the exchange profile), support from the third party is available for recovery and regaining access to the funds, since the private key remains in their possession. Among the wallet types discussed above, web wallets and mobile wallets are very often custodial, while it is rare for a desktop wallet to function as such.
- Non-custodial wallets: the user has exclusive ownership of the keys and therefore has total control over them. This type of wallet is more secure, especially when holding a large amount of cryptocurrency, and aligns with the decentralization principles that underpin cryptocurrencies. In relation to the previous categories, desktop wallets are normally non-custodial wallets and, by definition, so are cold wallets.

Finally, wallets can also be distinguished by their ability to support one or more cryptocurrencies, a classification that can overlap with those previously described:

- Single-currency wallet: a wallet that supports only one cryptocurrency (e.g. Electrum, mentioned earlier, which supports Bitcoin only).
- Multi-currency wallet: a wallet that supports multiple cryptocurrencies simultaneously (e.g. Exodus, mentioned earlier, which supports hundreds of cryptocurrencies).

As outlined above, wallets allow users to generate a private key, which in turn produces a public key and an address. Since common practice is to generate a new address and corresponding private key for every transaction, for privacy and security reasons, this can result in a large number of keys to manage and back up, with the risk that some may be lost. For this reason, almost all mainstream wallets are deterministic wallets, meaning they derive all private keys from a single seed, which is a randomly generated number typically represented as a list of 12 to 24 mnemonic words. Knowing the seed is sufficient to recover all associated keys, and it also allows for straightforward wallet migration between different implementations. It is therefore essential to record the seed words in a secure location and keep them strictly private, as they represent the only means of recovering one's funds in the event of loss or device failure. The most advanced form of deterministic wallet is the Hierarchical Deterministic (HD) wallet, which organizes keys in a tree structure. A parent key can derive a sequence of child keys, each of which can in turn derive grandchild keys, and so on indefinitely.

Returning to the example of Alice and Bob, the transaction process works as follows. Alice opens her wallet (in this case a desktop application such as Electrum) that holds the private key controlling her funds. She enters Bob's Bitcoin address, which Bob has previously shared with her, and the amount she wishes to send. The wallet then automatically signs the transaction using Alice's private key, proving that she is the legitimate owner of the funds, and broadcasts it to the Bitcoin network for validation.

1.3 Blockchain Nodes

Blockchain nodes are computers that run the Bitcoin Core or similar implementations and are the building blocks of the Bitcoin decentralized system. The higher the number of independent nodes, the higher the degree of decentralization and security.

Overall, the main role of nodes is to validate incoming transactions by verifying their correctness, append them to their local copy of the ledger, and propagate the new information across the network so that all other nodes can update their records accordingly.

Depending on the function they serve, nodes can be classified as follows:

- Full nodes: nodes that store a full and up-to-date copy of the blockchain transactions on their computer. Because they have the complete transaction history, they can autonomously verify the validity of transactions without requesting information from other nodes. Specifically, once a transaction is broadcast from a wallet, receiving full nodes check (i) whether the digital signature complies with the

public key of the address sending the bitcoins, (ii) whether the bitcoins have not already been spent in other transactions, and (iii) whether the transaction satisfies the Bitcoin protocol standard rules in general. After this preliminary legitimacy check, full nodes build a pool of unconfirmed transactions called "mempool", where transactions wait to be processed. Running a full node requires a large amount of disk space on the computer. As of December 2025, the required space exceeds 700 gigabytes of storage. Because of this significant requirement, there is also the option to avoid downloading the entire Bitcoin transaction history, discarding data that is not necessary for validating transactions. This configuration is called a pruned node and requires far less space on the computer's local storage.
- Lightweight nodes: also called Simplified Payment Verification (SPV) nodes, they do not participate in the validation process in the same way full nodes do, as they download only a portion of the block data rather than the complete blockchain. Instead, they request specific information from full nodes about particular transactions in order to reconstruct the balance of an address or to verify whether a transaction has been correctly included in the blockchain. Examples of lightweight nodes are wallets that broadcast transactions to the network. Since the storage space required to run such nodes is very low, they can easily be downloaded on laptops or mobile devices.
- Miner nodes: although themselves full nodes, miner nodes represent an important separate category due to one additional and crucial function: the creation of new blocks. They are the network participants responsible for collecting unconfirmed transactions into a block and demonstrating to the rest of the network their commitment to honest record-keeping, through a competitive and resource-intensive process named Proof of Work (PoW), as will be discussed in detail in Sect. 1.4. Every miner is therefore necessarily a full node, though not every full node is a miner. An exception arises in the case of mining pools, where individual miners contribute their computing power to a shared server rather than operating independently, collectively completing the Proof of Work and splitting the resulting block reward. In such arrangements, however, the pool administrator must operate as a full node. Today, the vast majority of miners participate in pools, as the computational difficulty of the Proof of Work has grown to the point where solo mining offers little realistic chance of earning the block reward.

Returning to our example, Alice's transaction in favor of Bob will be received by full nodes, which verify whether Alice's balance is sufficient to cover the transfer, whether those funds have not already been spent, and whether the transaction carries a valid digital signature. If the transaction passes these checks, it enters the mempool, which is essentially a waiting list for transactions pending inclusion in a block. Miners then select transactions from the mempool, group them into a block, and compete against one another to add it to the blockchain by solving a complex mathematical problem that demands specialized hardware and significant energy expenditure. This competitive process is known as the Proof of Work.

1.4 Transaction, Block Structure and Consensus Protocol

Before detailing the mechanism of the Proof of Work consensus protocol, it is important to further explore some elements that characterize a Bitcoin transaction and the way how it is included in a block of data.

Up to this point, we have spoken of transferring a certain amount of bitcoin from the balance of an address. In Bitcoin, however, the concept of a balance does not exist at the protocol level, as it is computed by the wallet by scanning the blockchain and aggregating all relevant transaction data. The fundamental unit is the Unspent Transaction Output (UTXO), which represents discrete amounts of bitcoin received at an address and not yet spent. A wallet derives the balance by summing all the UTXOs linked to a given address.

To better understand this concept, let us return to the example of the transaction between Alice and Bob. We established that Alice had previously received 1 bitcoin, which represents one UTXO. Because Alice sends 1 bitcoin to Bob, she consumes the entirety of that UTXO, which in turn creates a new UTXO for Bob's address. In the case where Alice had instead received 2 bitcoins from a previous transaction, she would hold a UTXO of 2 bitcoins. The transaction would proceed differently in this case, because UTXOs must be spent in their entirety within a single transaction. The wallet would therefore use Alice's entire UTXO as the transaction input, and the output would consist of 1 bitcoin sent to Bob and 1 bitcoin returned to Alice's address as change, which itself constitutes a new UTXO recorded on the blockchain. If, on the other hand, Alice held her 1 bitcoin across multiple UTXOs, for example one of 0.3 bitcoin, one of 0.2 bitcoin, and one of 0.5 bitcoin, the transaction to Bob would have required all three as inputs. Both scenarios can be observed in the following real example taken from a blockchain explorer.[5] Fig. 1.3 shows a transaction with a single input of $343,440 worth of bitcoin, of which $542.75 is sent to another address while the remaining $342,890 is returned to the sender as change. The two resulting outputs, $542.75 and $342,890, each constitute a new UTXO that will be spent in full in a subsequent transaction.

Figure 1.4 illustrates a different scenario, in which 102 separate UTXOs are consumed as inputs in favor of a single output of $377,299. As the inputs are spent in their entirety, no change output is generated.

A careful reader may have noticed that the total value of the UTXOs consumed does not convert entirely into output UTXOs, as a small portion is retained. This difference is known as the transaction fee, an important element of every transaction. It remunerates miners for adding the transaction to the blockchain and discourages attempts to flood the network with spurious transactions. Importantly, the fee is not a function of the amount transacted, but is instead proportional to the number of bytes the transaction occupies in the block.[6]

[5] A blockchain explorer is a search engine that allows users to view at a high level the data recorded on a blockchain.

[6] The size in bytes of a transaction increases with the number of inputs and outputs it entails.

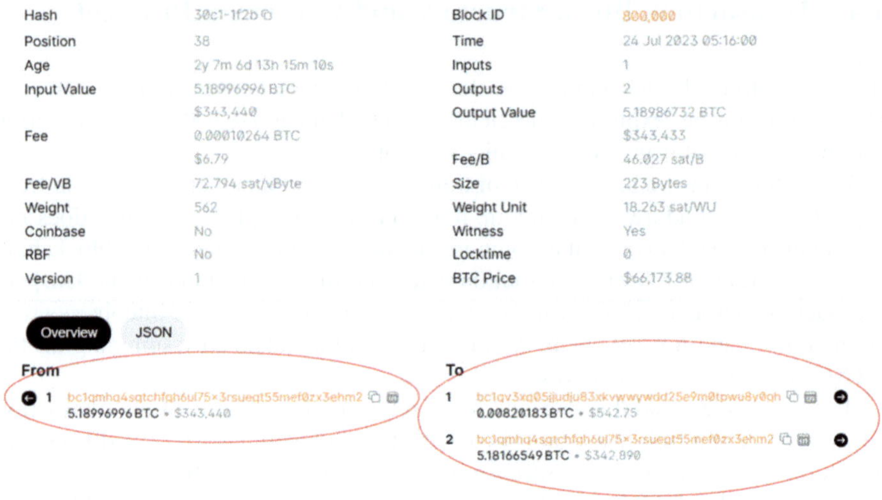

Fig. 1.3 Bitcoin block number 800,000, transaction hash ID 30c13bca5630e8655c20027474a309280272edcf4328af5f469272be3d901f2b. Source: Blockchain.com

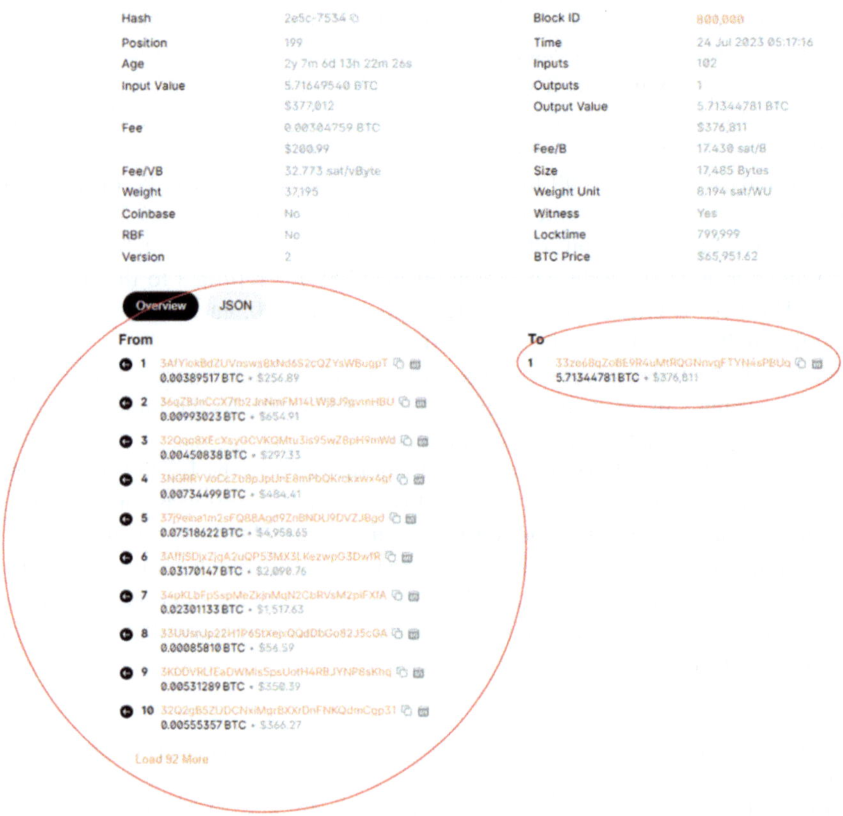

Fig. 1.4 Bitcoin block number 800,000, transaction hash ID 2e5cd15500a8eb6868e9190071659ec743e6ef83fdce8e86a1728f8cfa307534. Source: Blockchain.com

The fee is not the only incentive miners receive. They are also rewarded for processing transactions correctly through the coinbase transaction, a special transaction automatically generated by the Bitcoin protocol that sends a predetermined amount of newly created bitcoin to the miner as compensation for their work. It appears as the first transaction in every block and is only awarded to the miner successfully completes the Proof of Work. But what exactly does this entail, and why does it serve as a guarantee of honesty?

The Proof of Work consists in computing a hash value[7] of the block of data, based on certain parameters dictated by the block of transactions being processed, and requires hardware with significant computational power to carry out this task. This activity is a competition among miners, so only the miner or mining pool that first arrives at the solution can claim the reward. The others will stop searching for the hash value of the data block and will start over with a new block. Since the equipment required for mining consumes a large amount of electrical energy, miners face a very high opportunity cost if they attempt to falsify transactions. Indeed, once a block is submitted, the other nodes verify its validity, and any block containing fraudulent transactions is rejected by the network, causing the dishonest miner to forfeit both the fees and the coinbase reward, which would therefore not compensate them for the electrical energy consumed by their devices. Thanks to this balance of incentives and disincentives, the system finds its stability in a decentralized context.

To better understand how the mathematical proof that miners must deliver works in detail, it is necessary to illustrate how a block of transactions is composed.

A block of transactions is assembled by miners who select transactions from the mempool and consolidate them into a single data structure. Miners naturally favor transactions with a higher fee-to-byte ratio in order to maximize their earnings per block, which has an effective size limit of approximately 4 megabytes, though the average real block size ranges between 1 and 2 megabytes.[8] The block is normally made up of a header, which includes the block metadata on which the hash value of the block will be generated, followed by a list of transactions, which typically number in the thousands. The block header is composed of the following elements:

- Protocol version: a number that signals which consensus rules the block follows and which upgrades the miner who mined the block supports.

[7] The SHA-256 hash function is the algorithm used in Bitcoin's mining process. It transforms any piece of information into a string of 256 bits or 64 hexadecimal characters that cannot be converted back to its original form. For example, the hash value of "cryptocurrency" is "a81246023e3f6 c6167a08ba224409026f88bb8e98ed1431cd53cb63a328c6e84". If anything changes, the hash function returns a completely different hash. For example, the hash value of "cryptocurrency$" is "7b784d553c02e2f38367bf1a224341f08a44ef14e34167aa743aac2ac88c3596". The inverse process, however, is not feasible. This feature of hash functions means that the only way to produce a hash result matching a specific target is to try again and again, randomly modifying the input until the desired hash result appears by chance.

[8] https://ycharts.com/indicators/bitcoin_average_block_size

- Previous block hash: a 256 bit hash value calculated on the header of the previous block, also called the parent block. Because each block contains the hash of its parent, all blocks are linked back to the first genesis block and cannot be tampered with, as any alteration would change the hash value and therefore the entire chain, making such manipulation computationally infeasible.
- Merkle root: a 256 bit hash value that summarizes all the transactions in the block. It is calculated by hashing each transaction and aggregating pairs of hashes until a single hash, the Merkle root, is reached.
- Timestamp: the time of creation of the candidate block, expressed as the number of seconds elapsed since the first of January 1970 (known as the Unix Timestamp).
- Difficulty target: a hash value expressed in a compressed format that indicates the maximum permissible hash value of the block that must be found. The complexity of this value is adjusted every 2016 blocks by the Bitcoin protocol, such that on average, a miner can find the block hash every 10 min.
- Nonce: an arbitrary number that miners use to find the hash of the block in accordance with the target rule and therefore provide the Proof of Work.

A real example of a block header is depicted in Fig. 1.5 from the blockchain explorer Blockstream.info, where all the elements described above can be observed.

Based on these data, miners attempt by brute force to guess a valid hash value of the block, that is, a string of 64 hexadecimal characters. This hash value must be

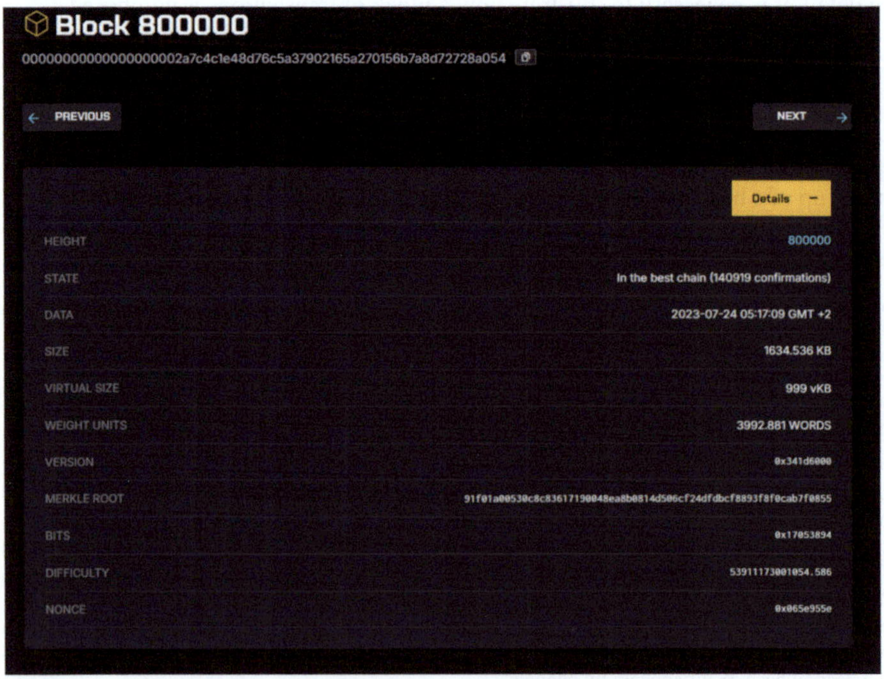

Fig. 1.5 Bitcoin block number 800,000, transaction. Source: Blockstream.info

equal to or lower than the target hash suggested by the protocol, which takes into account the computational power of the miners at any given moment, with the goal of spacing out the creation of a new blockchain block every 10 min. The target hash is characterized by a number of leading zeros at the beginning of the string, as this indicates a very small set of valid hash values, requiring billions of attempts to find one. The greater the number of leading zeros in the target, the smaller the set of valid hash combinations becomes. For example, the chance of generating a hash value with 19 leading zeros is 1 out of 75 billion trillion.

As of the 31st of December 2025, the target hash value in hexadecimal form is the following:

0000000000000000001e60500000000000000000000000000000000000000000

Hence, a valid hash for blocks minted on that date must be equal to or lower than that value. As proof, block number 930265, minted on 2025-12-31 at 12:32:27, has the following hash value:

000000000000000000006ff06c2cfa05a9784e88770b2b136942caa87fdeeae4

This value consistently has two additional leading zeros compared to the target and is therefore lower than it.

How is this value identified? The miner or pool of miners collects the transactions into the block, determines the header elements described earlier, namely the protocol version, the previous block hash, the Merkle root, the timestamp, and the hash target, and then tries different nonce values, thereby generating different hash values of the block header until one that satisfies the target is found. This is what, at a high level, encompasses the mining process and the Proof of Work.

Once a valid block hash is found, the block is broadcast to the other nodes, which verify both the validity of the transactions it contains and the correctness of the Proof of Work. This verification step is relatively straightforward. Since all elements, including the nonce, are already determined, nodes simply replicate the hash calculation and check whether it returns the expected value. If the block passes these checks, it achieves network consensus and is appended to the blockchain.

1.5 Forks

Let us now return to our initial example. Alice sends 1 bitcoin to Bob. We now know that a small portion of that bitcoin must be set aside for the fee, otherwise the transaction will likely never be processed. The transaction, having been validated by the nodes and entered into the mempool, is subsequently included in a candidate block by a miner. The miner sets the header values of that block and searches for the nonce such that the resulting hash value satisfies the target established by the protocol. Once that hash is found, the miner broadcasts the block to the other nodes, which verify its validity. If the block does not comply with the rules of the blockchain, it is rejected and the miner forfeits both the fees and the coinbase reward. The transaction between Alice and Bob returns to the mempool, ready to be processed again by another miner. If instead the block is valid, the nodes broadcast it to the entire network and update their local copies of the ledger. At this point, the other miners stop working on the previous block and begin mining a new one linked to the latest validated block. Alice and Bob will then see their transaction recorded on the blockchain and can consider it final once 6 additional blocks have been added on top of it, a threshold beyond which altering the chain becomes computationally infeasible.

This raises a question that has not yet been addressed. Why are 6 confirmations necessary? Because the blockchain could temporarily split into competing chains, and the block containing Alice and Bob's transaction could potentially be discarded. This phenomenon is known as a fork.

A first type of fork occurs very frequently and is caused by the temporary inconsistency of the ledger versions held by different nodes. It is fairly common for two miners to find a valid hash almost simultaneously, producing two different blocks that both point to the same parent block. At that moment the network finds itself with two valid versions of the chain, and nodes do not yet know which one to follow. New blocks will be added on top of each competing chain at different speeds, depending on how miners independently choose to proceed. The decision is consequently determined by the majority of miners, who will gradually concentrate their work on one of the two chains, making it longer than the other. As a general rule of the protocol, nodes follow the longest chain, synchronizing with the version of the ledger that incorporates the greatest amount of cumulative computational work. The logic behind this rule is that the longest chain represents the one on which the most computational work has been invested, making it statistically the most difficult to alter. The abandoned branch and its blocks become orphans, effectively excluded from the canonical chain, and the transactions they contained return to the mempool to await inclusion in a new block.

A fork can also result from malicious intent by miners seeking to attack the network, either by censoring valid transactions or by double-spending bitcoins. This occurs when miners controlling more than 51% of the network's computing power secretly build an alternative chain starting from a common block, in what is commonly known as a 51% attack. Such miners could spend bitcoins, wait for the transaction to appear in the publicly accepted chain, and then broadcast their privately built chain, which would be longer given their superior computational power, effectively reversing the original transaction. This would compromise the integrity of the payment system and cause users to lose confidence in it. This scenario is, however, considered unlikely, as the total computational power of the Bitcoin network today is extremely high, making it practically infeasible for any single party to accumulate the necessary resources. It is also worth noting that the scope of such an attack is limited. Malicious miners cannot move funds from wallets without authorization, as they have no access to the corresponding private keys, nor can they arbitrarily rewrite the blockchain beyond the most recent blocks. It is for this reason that 6 confirmation blocks are considered sufficient to regard a transaction as final and tamper-proof.

Finally, a fork can also arise from a change in protocol rules that is not unanimously adopted by all nodes. This is called a hard fork. Blockchain rules, such as block structure or consensus mechanisms, may need to be updated over time to address the evolving needs of the community or to correct limitations that have emerged in practice. Such changes cannot be implemented through an arbitrary software update but must be agreed upon by all network participants. If all nodes adopt the updated software, normal operations continue uninterrupted. If instead some nodes reject the changes, the blockchain splits into two branches: one continuing under the old rules and the other operating under the new ones. Miners and nodes that disagree will continue to process and validate blocks according to the old rules, and will not broadcast such blocks to those following the new rules, as these will no longer accept them. A concrete example of a Bitcoin hard fork is Bitcoin Cash, which emerged in August 2017 during the block size war (Bier, 2021), following the desire of part of the community to increase the block size to improve transaction scalability. The initial proposal raised the limit from 1 megabyte to 8 megabytes, later expanded to 32 megabytes. Anyone holding bitcoin at the time of the split automatically received an equivalent amount of bitcoin cash. This cryptocurrency remains operational today. A different example is Bitcoin Gold, which split from the Bitcoin chain in October 2017. Its goal was to modify the Proof of Work algorithm to make mining feasible on ordinary home computers, lowering the barrier to entry for individual participants and thereby improving the decentralization of the network.

1.6 The Blockchain Trilemma

Up to this point we have examined how Bitcoin works. As discussed, the architecture designed by Nakamoto was conceived to create electronic money used as a medium of exchange. However, this architecture has one significant problem: Bitcoin is not scalable. Since the mining difficulty is calibrated such that a block is found every 10 minutes on average and the block size is limited, when the volume of transactions requested by users increases, the system becomes congested. This leads to higher transaction costs and reduces the attractiveness of the network as a payment infrastructure (Zhou et al., 2020).

This problem is not easy to solve. Vitalik Buterin, the founder of Ethereum, coined and popularized the term "blockchain trilemma", which refers to the technological and architectural challenge of building a blockchain that is simultaneously secure, decentralized, and scalable. Bitcoin achieves a good degree of decentralization and security, but sacrifices scalability. To address this problem, many developers have sought to modify the protocol rules, particularly by studying alternative consensus mechanisms beyond Proof of Work. Proof of Work theoretically guarantees security and decentralization at the cost of scalability, both in terms of block production speed and block size. For instance, reducing Bitcoin's block interval below 10 minutes would allow the network to process transactions faster, but would also increase the frequency of forks, destabilizing the system and undermining its security. Conversely, increasing the block size would raise the storage requirements to run a node, reducing the decentralization of the network.

For this reason, several alternative consensus protocols have been developed to address the scalability limitations of Proof of Work. Among them, the most widely adopted by other cryptocurrencies are the following:

- Proof of Stake (PoS): PoS replaces the competitive hashing process among miners with a system in which a single selected validator computes the block hash. Specifically, validators express their willingness to propose a new block by staking the blockchain's native currency. The protocol then selects a validator with a degree of randomness, though the probability of selection increases with the amount staked. If the validator acts against the protocol rules, the block is rejected by the other nodes and the validator loses part of their stake as a penalty, forfeiting the block reward as well. The disincentive is therefore not the sunk cost of energy expenditure, as in Proof of Work, but an economic one, as validators put their own holdings at risk to prove their honesty.
  Since the computational difficulty of producing a valid hash is negligible, energy consumption is minimal, making Proof of Stake significantly more environmentally friendly than its predecessor. In Proof of Work, all miners compete simultaneously to validate the same block, consuming energy regardless of whether they win the reward. This energy expenditure is predominantly sourced from fossil fuels (de Vries, 2019), making the protocol highly polluting. Indeed, estimates indicate that Bitcoin's energy consumption alone is equivalent to the entire annual electricity usage of Sweden, with CO_2 emissions comparable to those of Greece and Oman combined (Kohli et al., 2023).
  In line with the blockchain trilemma, however, Proof of Stake improves scalability at the cost of some decentralization, as the concentration of coins among a small number of wealthy participants may translate into a concentration of decision-making power. Ethereum is a prominent example of a blockchain using Proof of Stake, having transitioned from Proof of Work in September 2022.
- Delegated Proof of Stake (DPoS): DPoS is a variation of PoS in which block validators are elected by coin holders from a limited set of candidates known as delegates. For each block, coin holders cast votes weighted proportionally to their staked holdings. The most voted candidate is selected to process the transactions and earn the reward, which is then distributed among supporting voters. If the elected validator behaves dishonestly, voters can redirect their support to other candidates, excluding the delegate from future block creation. This protocol further increases transaction speed but reduces decentralization, as only a small subset of nodes can serve as block creators. TRON is a prominent example of a blockchain employing DPoS.

As of December 2025, about 60% of the cryptocurrencies tracked by cryptoslate.com employ a Proof of Work consensus protocol, whereas 15% and 3% use Proof of Stake and Delegated Proof of Stake respectively. Other protocols exist but are less commonly used, such as Proof of Authority (PoA), Practical Byzantine Fault

Tolerance (PBFT), Proof of Burn (PoB), and Proof of Space (PoSpace), among others. Some blockchains also operate using a hybrid format combining Proof of Work and Proof of Stake, drawing advantages from both. Peercoin is an example of a blockchain using such a hybrid protocol.

Modifying the consensus protocol alone, however, may offer only partial improvements. Other solutions aimed at enhancing blockchain scalability include the development of Layer 2 protocols and sidechains. So far, we have discussed Bitcoin and briefly mentioned other cryptocurrencies with their own blockchain, such as Ethereum. These blockchains, which have their own native currency and consensus rules, are referred to as Layer 1 solutions. On the other hand, layer 2 solutions are applications built on top of Layer 1 blockchains to extend their functionality. They rely on the security provided by the underlying Layer 1 protocol and handle certain operations off-chain, thereby reducing the workload on the main blockchain. The most notable Layer 2 solutions are the following:

- Payment channels: solutions that enable faster and more efficient transactions. Users open off-chain payment channels by locking a certain amount of digital currency on the main blockchain through a funding transaction. Once the channel is active, payments can be exchanged almost instantly and at minimal cost. Channels can also be interconnected, so transactions may occur even between parties that do not share a direct channel, as long as a path exists through other users. Similar to the blockchain, the architecture of these solutions includes mechanisms that remove any incentive for counterparties to act dishonestly. A channel can be closed at any time either by mutual agreement or unilaterally, and the resulting net position is recorded on the blockchain through a settlement transaction. An example of a payment channel solution for Bitcoin is the Lightning Network (Poon & Dryja, 2016).
- Rollups: solutions that process transactions off-chain and periodically submit a compressed record of them to the main blockchain, reducing congestion on the Layer 1 and lowering fees for users. There are two types of rollups:
  - Optimistic rollups: they take their name from the assumption that off-chain transactions are valid by default. Their correctness is not verified automatically upon submission to the blockchain but can be challenged by any network participant within a designated challenge period. If a disputed transaction is found to be invalid, it is corrected on the blockchain. This mechanism introduces a delay in the effective availability of funds, as users must wait for the challenge period to expire before their funds are considered final. An example of an optimistic rollup for Ethereum is Arbitrum.
  - Zero knowledge rollups: by contrast, they verify the correctness of off-chain transactions before they are submitted to the Layer 1. This verification produces a cryptographic proof of validity that accompanies the compressed transaction data included in the block. Because the validity of the submitted data is mathematically guaranteed, there is no challenge period and funds are available immediately. However, the generation of these proofs is

computationally intensive and tends to centralize the role of the node managing Layer 2 transactions. An example for Ethereum is ZKsync.

Unlike the previous scaling solutions, sidechains improve the throughput of a Layer 1 blockchain without relying on it for security or consensus. Each sidechain is an independent blockchain that operates under its own protocol and rules, connected to the main chain through a two-way peg that allows digital assets to be transferred between the two in both directions. The mechanism works through a lock-and-mint process. When a user wants to move assets to the sidechain, those assets are locked on the main chain and an equivalent amount of tokens is created on the sidechain to represent them. Transactions can then take place faster and more cheaply, since the sidechain operates under typically less restrictive consensus rules. When the user wants to return to the main chain, the sidechain tokens are burned and the original assets are unlocked. One drawback of this approach is that, unlike Layer 2 solutions, sidechains do not inherit the security guarantees of the main blockchain. An example of a Bitcoin sidechain is the Liquid Network.

The scaling solutions discussed in this section represent the most prominent attempts to address the blockchain trilemma. As the ecosystem continues to grow, particularly following the innovations brought by smart contracts, further developments in this area are to be expected.

1.7 From Payments to Smart Contracts

In the preceding sections, the mechanisms underlying Bitcoin and, more broadly, the general infrastructure shared across cryptocurrencies have been examined in detail. As illustrated, bitcoin was conceived as a means of payment, with the objective of replacing centralized institutions that issue fiat currencies and establishing itself as the future of the payment system. Yet after nearly two decades, traditional means of payment remain dominant, which raises the question of what explains this outcome.

For an asset to qualify as a currency, it must fulfil three distinct functions:

- Medium of exchange
- Unit of account
- Store of value

Bitcoin possesses the requisite attributes to function as a medium of exchange, being fungible, durable, and resistant to counterfeiting. It has also demonstrated properties consistent with a store of value, having appreciated considerably in overall terms since its inception, despite significant price volatility. However, it fails to fulfill the function of a unit of account. Given that its price can fluctuate substantially even over short time horizons, bitcoin does not maintain the valuation stability relative to other goods that such a function demands. For this reason, the academic literature has repeatedly concluded that bitcoin is ill-suited to serve as a currency in the conventional sense (Baur & Dimpfl, 2021). This raises the question: what purpose does bitcoin serve, and more broadly, what can cryptocurrencies offer as an asset class?

Beyond payments, many have recognized that the blockchain can be employed for broader applications. One important example is the notary function. In Bitcoin, it is indeed possible to represent digital assets on the blockchain by inscribing metadata within a new output included in a transaction, through the operational code OP_RETURN. Such metadata could represent, for example, the transfer of ownership of a stock from one individual to another. One of the earliest applications of this kind were "colored coins", digital certificates inscribed on the Bitcoin blockchain that certain software built on top of Bitcoin was able to read and track in terms of the movement of such digital assets. This application never gained significant traction within the Bitcoin community, however, as such outputs do not create UTXOs but nonetheless occupy space within the transaction and consequently within the block. For this reason, there has been considerable resistance among nodes to processing such transactions, which are seen as atypical of Bitcoin's primary role and as contributing to network congestion.

Similarly, a blockchain can also permit the construction of contracts between two or more parties, which can be inscribed and stored without the possibility of modification. These are known as smart contracts, which can be defined as programs that operate on distributed ledger technology and whose execution automatically binds two or more parties according to predefined terms.

In Bitcoin, the possibility of deploying such contracts is very limited. Its blockchain can only execute certain standard scripts with elementary functions, such as simple evaluations of spending conditions, due to the fact that Bitcoin is built with a non-Turing-complete scripting language and therefore does not support complex operations. Attempts were made to use OP_RETURN to insert metadata relating to smart contracts executable on secondary layers of the blockchain. However, due to the space limitations of the OP_RETURN operator and the resistance of the community to using block space for such purposes, these solutions never gained significant enthusiasm or adoption (Caldarelli, 2023).

Following a strong desire to explore the new functionalities derivable from blockchain technology, many developers worked on building new ecosystems capable of overcoming the limitations that Bitcoin imposed on such innovations. It was out of this effort that Ethereum was born in 2015. Ethereum is a programmable blockchain that functions as a decentralized computer, in which complex code can be deployed and executed in the form of smart contracts. Ethereum shares several foundational characteristics with Bitcoin. Both rely on a chain of blocks containing transactions processed by nodes according to predefined consensus rules, authenticated through digital signatures, and supported by a native cryptocurrency, namely ether in the case of Ethereum. The two platforms, however, differ substantially in purpose and architecture. Bitcoin is designed to record and transfer value between peers, storing a history of transactions over time. Ethereum, by contrast, operates as a stateful computational environment, storing both data and code, tracking their evolution across blocks, and designed not for transactional exchange but for the deployment and execution of smart contracts.

In the Ethereum ecosystem, two types of accounts exist. The first are Externally Owned Accounts (EOAs), controlled by private keys and used to initiate standard transactions, analogously to addresses in Bitcoin. The second are contract accounts, each identified by a unique address corresponding to a deployed smart contract and operating according to code rather than being controlled by a private key. As a consequence, contract accounts cannot initiate transactions independently, since only EOAs can originate them. They can, however, respond to incoming transactions by calling other contracts, allowing complex multi-step execution paths to be constructed. Anyone can deploy a smart contract on the Ethereum blockchain by sending a transaction containing the code, written primarily in the Solidity or Vyper programming languages, along with the constructor parameters required to initialize it. Once deployed, the contract is immutable, meaning its code cannot be altered, and it maintains its own ether balance. Rather than being owned by any external party, a smart contract account is in effect self-governing, since no individual holds a private key granting special protocol-level privileges over it, unless such privileges have been explicitly coded into the contract itself.

The execution of smart contracts is carried out by the Ethereum Virtual Machine (EVM), a decentralized computing environment run collectively by every node on the network. When a transaction is directed to a contract address, it triggers the execution of that contract within the EVM, using the transaction and any accompanying data as its input. This mechanism allows transactions to invoke specific functions of a contract, enabling a wide range of programmable behaviors, and with each new block the EVM updates the state of all active smart contracts accordingly (Antonopoulos et al., 2025).

To illustrate the potential of this technology, consider a smart contract designed to automate an insurance agreement, in which compensation is transferred to a beneficiary automatically upon the occurrence of a predefined condition, without any manual intervention. A recent real-world application of this kind can be found in the airline insurance industry, where flight delays or cancellations automatically trigger instant compensation to the ticket holder, bypassing the need for manual claims processing entirely (Shetty et al., 2022). Another concrete application has emerged in real estate asset management, where ownership stakes in properties are tokenized on blockchain and distributed to investors, who benefit from both capital appreciation and the automatic distribution of rental income, all managed through smart contracts. The use of tokens in this context makes real estate investment management considerably more efficient, flexible, and accessible compared to traditional vehicles such as REITs, while also enabling a much higher degree of fractional ownership (Kreppmeier et al., 2023). But how does a contract on Ethereum know if a flight is delayed or cancelled or whether a rental payment has been received?

An important actor in this regard is the oracle, a third-party service responsible for communicating off-chain information to the blockchain such as asset prices, meteorological data, or other external events upon which the logic of the smart contract depends. Since the oracle acts as the sole arbiter of the accuracy of the information it provides, it introduces an element of centralization into an otherwise decentralized system. The extent to which a smart contract can be trusted therefore depends not only on the integrity of the blockchain protocol, but also on the reliability of the oracle feeding it data. This issue is commonly referred to as the "oracle problem" and remains one of the most actively debated challenges in the smart contract space, although mechanisms aimed at reducing the incentive for oracles to behave dishonestly are currently being developed.

1.8 Tokens, Dapps and Web3

The rapid adoption of Ethereum and the enthusiasm of its community for having at their disposal a platform on which to deploy smart contracts freely brought blockchain technology to a new level of innovation. Increasingly sophisticated contracts began to emerge, aimed at managing fundraising, representing and exchanging digital assets on the blockchain, providing decentralised borrowing and lending services, and facilitating decentralized governance projects, among other functions. These contracts also typically involved the creation of a dedicated token, useful for managing and building the ecosystem of the project. Such tokens can represent ownership of an asset, grant access to a service or platform, or function as a means of exchange. Furthermore, smart contracts enabled the development of decentralized applications, laying the foundations of what has come to be known as Web3.

In the early stages, however, each developer wrote smart contracts according to their own style and design choices, resulting in a highly fragmented landscape with significant differences in structure and behavior from one contract to another. In order to bring uniformity to this space, minimize the risk of bugs leading to incorrect behavior, and establish a common framework for the interpretation of smart contracts, dedicated standards were introduced that remain widely used to this day. While it is technically possible to write a smart contract entirely from scratch, the use of established standards is strongly advisable given the risks associated with potential coding errors. The two most important standards implemented on Ethereum are:

- Ethereum Request for Comment 20 (ERC-20): the standard that establishes the principal rules for the creation of fungible tokens. The fungibility property of a token refers to its interchangeability and non-uniqueness, meaning that exchanging one token for another results in no meaningful difference. Ether, for instance, is fungible, as one unit is identical in value and function to any other unit.
  This standard was introduced in November 2015 to define the minimum mandatory rules that a smart contract must implement in order to issue tokens. Specifically, every ERC-20 compliant contract must implement the following minimum set of functions and properties:

  - totalSupply: a function that defines the total supply of tokens created, which can be either fixed or variable.
  - balanceOf: a function that returns the amount of tokens held by a given account.
  - transfer: a function that permits the transfer of a specified amount of tokens to an account.
  - transferFrom: a function that transfers a specified amount of tokens from one account to another.
  - approve: a function that grants permission to a third party to withdraw tokens from another account.
  - allowance: a function that returns the amount of tokens a spender address is permitted to withdraw from an owner address.
  - transfer: an event triggered whenever a successful transfer is made.
  - approval: an event emitted every time the approve function is called.

- Ethereum Request for Comment 721 (ERC-721): the standard that establishes the principal rules for the creation of non-fungible tokens (NFTs). These are tokens that are not interchangeable, as each one uniquely represents a specific item. An NFT can represent, for example, a digital collectible or proof of ownership of a physical or digital asset. A well-known example of digital collectibles are the Bored Ape digital drawings,[9] which during 2020 and 2021 gained considerable popularity and reached valuations of millions of US dollars. This standard was introduced in January 2018 and shares several functions and events with the ERC-20.

These token standards represent minimum specifications that must be adhered to when implementing smart contracts, though the code can always be extended with additional functions as needed. One advantage of using such established templates is that wallets, user platforms, and exchanges can recognize the token without requiring any update to their existing systems, allowing it to be immediately available for trading. Importantly, tokens are managed by smart contracts, meaning that token transfers do not occur as direct transactions on the Ethereum blockchain. Rather, transferring a token requires composing a transaction that calls a specific function of the smart contract. This operation requires a fee in ether, known as "gas", which compensates the network for the computational resources consumed in executing the contract.

The standardization of tokens and their relative ease of implementation also facilitated the development and widespread adoption of decentralized applications, commonly known as DApps. A DApp is essentially a smart contract paired with a web user interface that provides peer-to-peer infrastructure services. Traditional applications rely on proprietary closed-source logic, a centralized server for data storage, and a dedicated frontend through which users access the service. A DApp, by contrast, uses a smart contract to handle both the application logic and data

[9] https://opensea.io/collection/boredapeyachtclub

storage, while the frontend can in principle be built by anyone, although an official one typically exists. The key advantages of DApps stem from their decentralized nature. There is no single point of failure, as the application runs on the blockchain through the network of nodes whenever the smart contract is called. Nor is a centralized development team required to maintain it, as the application operates autonomously based on the logic encoded in the smart contract.

This shift away from centralized control over both data and application logic represents the foundational principle of what has come to be known as Web3, a vision of the internet in which services are no longer intermediated by a central authority but are instead openly accessible to anyone and governed by code rather than by institutions. A prominent example of a DApp is Uniswap, the most widely used decentralized exchange for cryptocurrencies and tokens. Like any centralized exchange, it is accessible through an official web frontend,[10] but the similarities end there. Rather than requiring users to register an account and entrust their funds to a centralized platform, as is the case with exchanges such as Binance or Coinbase, Uniswap allows users to connect their own wallet and trade digital assets directly through smart contracts deployed on the Ethereum blockchain. No intermediary holds the funds at any point, the platform requires no ongoing maintenance, and no central authority can suspend or interfere with its operations.

1.9 Conclusion

This chapter has provided a high-level overview of the main concepts underlying how cryptocurrencies and blockchain technology work. As the reader will have noticed, this topic sits at the intersection of several disciplines, which makes it less intuitive than many other subjects. Nevertheless, the fundamental mechanics of how transactions are validated, recorded, and secured on a decentralized network have now be outlined.

Importantly, it should be clear that cryptocurrencies are far from homogeneous. The developments that have followed the creation of Bitcoin demonstrate that they cannot be regarded exclusively as a medium of exchange in the conventional sense. Ethereum stands as the most compelling illustration of this point, showing how blockchain technology can accommodate and enhance real-world services, giving intrinsic value to the network and its native assets. In its wake, indeed, a broad ecosystem of cryptocurrencies has emerged, serving functions as diverse as asset tokenization, decentralized governance, and smart contract execution.

Due to this heterogeneity as well as their unique idiosyncratic risks, largely orthogonal to those of traditional asset classes, cryptocurrencies can be regarded as financial assets and as a new distinct asset class.

[10] The official frontend of Uniswap is https://app.uniswap.org/

References

Antonopoulos, A. M. (2017). *Mastering bitcoin: Programming the open blockchain* (2nd ed.). O'Reilly Media.

Antonopoulos, A. M., Parisi, C., Mazza, A., Pozzolini, N., & Wood, G. (2025). *Mastering Ethereum: Implementing smart contracts* (2nd ed.). O'Reilly Media.

Baur, D. G., & Dimpfl, T. (2021). The volatility of bitcoin and its role as a medium of exchange and a store of value. *Empirical Economics, 61*, 2663–2683. https://doi.org/10.1007/s00181-020-01990-5

Bier, J. (2021). *The blocksize war: The battle over who controls Bitcoin's protocol rules.*

Caldarelli, G. (2023). Before Ethereum. The origin and evolution of blockchain oracles. *IEEE Access, 11*, 50899–50917. https://doi.org/10.1109/ACCESS.2023.3279106

Chiu, J., & Koeppl, T. V. (2017). The economics of cryptocurrencies bitcoin and beyond. *SSRN Journal*. https://doi.org/10.2139/ssrn.3048124

de Vries, A. (2019). Renewable energy will not solve Bitcoin's sustainability problem. *Joule, 3*, 893–898. https://doi.org/10.1016/j.joule.2019.02.007

Kohli, V., Chakravarty, S., Chamola, V., Sangwan, K. S., & Zeadally, S. (2023). An analysis of energy consumption and carbon footprints of cryptocurrencies and possible solutions. *Digital Communications and Networks, 9*, 79–89. https://doi.org/10.1016/j.dcan.2022.06.017

Kreppmeier, J., Laschinger, R., Steininger, B. I., & Dorfleitner, G. (2023). Real estate security token offerings and the secondary market: Driven by crypto hype or fundamentals? *Journal of Banking & Finance, 154*, 106940. https://doi.org/10.1016/j.jbankfin.2023.106940

Lehar, A., & Parlour, C. A. (2019). *Liquidity demand and bitcoin transaction fees.*

Nakamoto, S. (2008). *Bitcoin: A peer-to-peer electronic cash system.* Satoshi Nakamoto Institute Website. https://nakamotoinstitute.org/library/bitcoin/.

Poon, J., & Dryja, T. (2016). *The bitcoin lightning network: Scalable off-chain instant payments.* https://cdn.nakamotoinstitute.org/docs/lightning-network.pdf

Sajter, D. (2022). Overseas transaction fees: Sending money via bitcoin vs. banks. *Zagreb International Review of Economics and Business, 25*, 65–83. https://doi.org/10.2478/zireb-2022-0025

Shetty, A., Shetty, A. D., Pai, R. Y., Rao, R. R., Bhandary, R., Shetty, J., Nayak, S., Keerthi Dinesh, T., & Dsouza, K. J. (2022). Block chain application in insurance services: A systematic review of the evidence. *SAGE Open, 12*, 21582440221079877. https://doi.org/10.1177/21582440221079877

Zhou, Q., Huang, H., Zheng, Z., & Bian, J. (2020). Solutions to scalability of blockchain: A survey. *IEEE Access, 8*, 16440–16455. https://doi.org/10.1109/ACCESS.2020.2967218

Chapter 2
Cryptocurrency Typologies and Classification

2.1 A Taxonomy of Cryptocurrency

The general term used to refer to a currency exchanged on a blockchain is "cryptocurrency," as it relies on cryptographic encryption and was originally conceived as a medium of exchange. In their early days, Bitcoin and similar ones were indeed simply called cryptocurrencies. As the space evolved, however, new forms of digital assets began to emerge, progressively expanding the terminology. The term "altcoin" was coined to refer to alternative cryptocurrencies created in an attempt to improve upon the way transaction value is digitally sent and received (Spurr & Ausloos, 2021). Then, following the creation of Ethereum and the ERC standards discussed in the previous chapter, "tokens" gained prominence, namely digital assets enforced by means of smart contracts that can represent the digitalization of economic value within an ecosystem (Freni et al., 2022), encompassing anything from a currency, to a voting right, a property right, or access to a product or service. So broad was this new category that people started referring to "cryptocurrencies" and "tokens" interchangeably, treating them as equivalent despite their fundamental differences. In other words, with each new wave of innovation and consequent new layer of terminology, over time this proliferation of names gave rise to growing conceptual confusion, as fundamentally different types of assets began to be referred to under the same umbrella term.

The most compelling instance of this confusion is the aforementioned habit of referring to tokens using the word "cryptocurrency," a term that was originally conceived to denote peer-to-peer electronic money. A fundamental distinction exists between the two. A cryptocurrency is a coin implied by its own blockchain, serving as the native incentive currency of the distributed ledger, whereas tokens are assets created on top of a blockchain and therefore do not constitute its native currency. This distinction carries significant implications for security, as tokens rely entirely on the blockchain on which they are deployed for their integrity, while

D. Sandretto, *Cryptocurrencies as an Asset Class*, SpringerBriefs in Finance,
https://doi.org/10.1007/978-3-032-31491-8_2

cryptocurrencies are by definition an intrinsic part of the security of the protocol they underpin, being the currency used to operate the transactions of their own network. Nonetheless, beyond these important formal differences, the word "cryptocurrency" continues to be widely used in practice as a catch-all term for all digital assets whose functioning is governed by DLT technology.

For the purposes of a correct classification, however, a more precise and rigorous taxonomy is required. Regardless of whether one is referring to a digital currency, a digital coin, a cryptocurrency, or a token, a broader inclusive term is needed. Drawing inspiration from regulators, we can identify that term in "cryptoasset," defined as any digital asset issued via blockchain technology. This broader definition has been extensively adopted by regulatory authorities, such as the European Union (2023) with the MiCA regulation and the Basel Committee on Banking Supervision (2022) with the Cryptoasset Exposures framework. As stated in the Basel Cryptoasset Exposures framework at article 60.1:

> Cryptoassets are defined as private digital assets that depend on cryptography and distributed ledger technologies (DLT) or similar technologies. Digital assets are a digital representation of value, which can be used for payment or investment purposes or to access a good or service.

The definition is intentionally broad and captures all the different value propositions that digital assets are set to entail. From this point forward in this chapter, we will therefore refer to cryptocurrencies and tokens using the more general and inclusive term "cryptoasset."

2.2 A Categorization of Cryptoassets

Given the different infrastructures and functionalities that cryptoassets entail, this section provides an extensive classification based on such characteristics. This is important from an investment perspective, as knowing the major functionality or typology of a cryptoasset allows one to understand its intrinsic value. Unfortunately, the nature of cryptoassets can sometimes overlap, since it ultimately depends on the use that the holder makes of them. For example, Ether, the cryptoasset native to the Ethereum blockchain, can be employed for payments if a user wishes to do so, but its primary function is to enable the deployment of smart contracts. Therefore, in the classification proposed here, each cryptoasset is evaluated based on the objective function it is designed to serve, abstracting from the subjective use that individuals may make of it.

The classification also draws from the existing literature and from the efforts of regulators who have repeatedly attempted to classify cryptoassets into broader or narrower categories (Eska et al., 2025; Fry & Ibiloye, 2023; Härdle et al., 2020). Given the rapid pace at which the space continues to evolve, however, existing frameworks often fall short of capturing the full spectrum of functionalities that cryptoassets currently exhibit, making a more precise classification necessary.

While any such attempt will inevitably become outdated over time, the one proposed here is designed to be sufficiently inclusive of the macro-level functionalities that characterize the ecosystem today.

The classification proposed consists of the following types of cryptoassets: Payment, Infrastructure, Security, Stablecoins, NFT and Utility.

2.2.1 Payment Cryptoassets

The first category consists of cryptoassets created and intended for payment purposes, encompassing both coins native to their own blockchain, such as Bitcoin, and tokens whose primary purpose is transactional in nature, although the latter are less common. These assets are designed to function essentially as a medium of exchange, and their value is naturally tied to the degree of adoption they achieve as a means of payment. Representative examples of this category include Bitcoin, Litecoin, Monero and Shiba Inu. As Bitcoin has been extensively covered in the previous chapter, it will not be discussed further here.

Litecoin Litecoin is a peer-to-peer digital currency that enables near-instantaneous transactions at negligible cost to anyone, anywhere in the world. It was created in 2011 and released under the MIT/X11 open-source license. Its network operates without any central authority, relying instead on cryptographic mathematics to secure transactions, and its software is distributed transparently, allowing for independent verification of the source code by anyone who wishes to inspect it, just like Bitcoin. Inspired by the latter, the Litecoin blockchain introduces meaningful improvements to the transaction validation process. Most notably, it targets a block generation time of 2.5 minutes, compared to Bitcoin's 10, resulting in significantly faster payment confirmations. Rather than Bitcoin's SHA-256, Litecoin employs the Scrypt hashing algorithm, a memory-intensive proof-of-work function that makes dedicated mining hardware considerably more complex to develop. The network also supports a maximum supply of 84 million coins, four times greater than Bitcoin's, providing a broader base of units for everyday transactional use. Litecoin has found adoption in everyday commerce and is accepted by thousands of businesses globally through payment processors such as BitPay, while platforms like Bitrefill allow users to purchase gift cards and pay bills directly with their holdings. As of the end of December 2025, it is ranked 19th by market capitalization.

Monero Monero is a particularly interesting example of a payment cryptoasset, as it is a privacy-focused digital currency whose blockchain does not publicly disclose details about the transactions occurring on its network. Its blockchain was launched in April 2014 under a proof-of-work consensus protocol. A new block is created every 2 minutes, and rather than enforcing a fixed maximum block size, the protocol relies on a dynamic block size combined with a block reward penalty mechanism, ensuring that scalability adapts to demand over time. It leverages a payment system that is fast, efficient, and anonymous by default. The sender, receiver, and amount of every single transaction are concealed through the use of three core cryptographic technologies. Stealth Addresses ensure that each payment is sent to a unique, one-time address that only the recipient can identify, making it impossible for outside observers to link transactions to a known public address. Ring Signatures hide the sender by mixing the real signing key with a set of other public keys from the blockchain, making it impossible to determine which party actually authorized the transaction. RingCT, short for Ring Confidential Transactions, conceals the amounts involved by recording a cryptographic commitment to the value rather than the value itself, while still allowing the network to verify that no new money is being created out of thin air.[1] The combined result of these three mechanisms is that on the Monero blockchain it is impossible to know who sent what to whom and for how much. However, this feature represents a double-edged sword, as the anonymity of transactions has led to its use in illicit activities, including money laundering. As of the end of December 2025, it is ranked 15th by market capitalization.

Shiba Inu Shiba Inu is a cryptoasset created using the ERC-20 standard on the Ethereum blockchain and is one of the most well-known meme coins in the world. Meme coins are cryptoassets born out of internet culture, irony, or humor, with no predefined technical or financial function. For this reason, their only concrete use case is to serve as a pure medium of exchange, meaning they can be used as a currency in the traditional sense, to the extent that a community of users voluntarily chooses to adopt them for transactions. This is precisely why they are classified under this category. Shiba Inu was created in 2020 as an explicit replica of another well-known meme coin, Dogecoin. Both take their name and imagery from the same Japanese dog breed, and both share an origin devoid of serious technical ambitions. The main difference between the two is that Dogecoin has its own independent blockchain, based on a modified version of Litecoin, while Shiba Inu was issued directly on the Ethereum blockchain as an ERC-20 token, inheriting all of its consensus mechanisms. The total supply of Shiba Inu is fixed at one quadrillion tokens, an astronomically large number that explains the extremely low unit price, typically in the range of fractions of a cent, and its entire issuance and distribution logic is governed by the original smart contract. As of the end of December 2025, it is ranked 26th by market capitalization.

2.2.2 *Infrastructure Cryptoassets*

Infrastructure cryptoassets are the native assets of blockchain networks that provide the foundational layer on which decentralized applications, smart contracts, and other cryptoassets are built. Their value is tied to the usage and security of the

[1] For more on Monero, an interested reader is referred to Alonso and Koe's (2018) whitepaper.

underlying network, since the asset is used to call smart contract functions and more generally to allow the ecosystem to function correctly. This category includes cryptoassets linked to blockchains such as Ethereum, Solana and Polkadot. As Ethereum has been described in the previous chapter, the following section proceeds directly to the remaining examples.

Solana Solana is a blockchain similar to Ethereum that enables faster and cheaper transactions through its native cryptoasset SOL, and that allows the creation of tokens following a standard analogous to Ethereum's ERC standards, here referred to as SPL, which stands for Solana Program Library. Solana was launched in March 2020 with the goal of providing a faster infrastructure that is more resilient to network congestion compared to other blockchains such as Ethereum. It introduces the Proof of History, a consensus mechanism that regulates the flow of validated blocks through a cryptographic clock that sequences them, resulting in lower delays in the construction of the blockchain as communication between nodes is streamlined by this mechanism. Block validation is however managed through Proof of Stake, meaning that validators are required to stake SOL in order to participate in block creation. Proof of History operates alongside this process, resulting in a hybrid consensus mechanism. Thanks to this configuration, Solana is theoretically capable of processing at least 65,000 transactions per second (Thakur, 2025), making it one of the fastest blockchains on the market. For this reason, it has become, together with Ethereum, one of the most widely used blockchains for creating tokens and building decentralized applications, and it is currently ranked 7th by market capitalization.

Polkadot Polkadot is a blockchain launched in 2020 by Gavin Wood, one of the co-founders of Ethereum, with the goal of solving one of the most fundamental limitations of existing blockchain infrastructure, namely the inability of independent blockchains to communicate and share resources with one another. In principle, it is not possible to transfer a cryptoasset native to one blockchain directly onto another. For instance, Ether cannot be used natively on Solana, and vice versa. Workarounds do exist, most notably wrapped tokens, which are synthetic representations of a cryptoasset issued on a foreign blockchain and pegged to the value of the original. However, this process requires the use of bridges, which are third-party protocols that lock the original asset on its native chain and mint a corresponding wrapped version elsewhere, introducing additional complexity, trust assumptions, and security risks. Polkadot was designed to make this kind of cross-chain communication native and trustless, without relying on external bridges. Its native cryptoasset is DOT, which is used for staking, governance, and participation in the network's slot auction mechanism.

Unlike Ethereum or Solana, Polkadot is not designed to be a single fast chain but rather a multi-chain network. Its architecture revolves around a central blockchain called the Relay Chain, which provides shared security and consensus to the entire system, and a set of independent blockchains called parachains, which connect to the Relay Chain and inherit its security without needing to build their own validator network from scratch. Each parachain can have its own logic, token standard, and governance model, while still benefiting from the security of the broader Polkadot network. Communication between parachains happens natively through a protocol called XCM, which stands for Cross-Consensus Messaging, and which allows assets and data to be transferred across chains without relying on external bridges. For its consensus mechanism, Polkadot uses a variant of Proof of Stake called Nominated Proof of Stake, in which validators are elected by nominators who delegate their DOT to support specific validators. Dishonest behavior is penalized through a slashing mechanism that affects both the validator and its nominators. As of the end of December 2025, it is ranked 33rd by market capitalization.

2.2.3 Security Cryptoasset

The third typology of cryptoasset refers to those that resemble securities. Drawing from the definition provided by Lambert et al. (2022), a security cryptoasset "is a digital representation of an investment product, recorded on a distributed ledger, subject to regulation under securities laws". More substantively, they are investment products analogous to traditional financial instruments (e.g. stocks and bonds), and thus typically confer cash flow rights to investors and, in some cases, also voting rights. Since they are representations of underlying assets, these cryptoassets are by definition tokens issued on blockchains such as Ethereum via ERC standards or Solana via SPL standards, and their value can be calculated in the same way as any traditional financial asset.

These cryptoassets are subject to legal compliance requirements, as investment products must adhere to regulations governing public distribution and investor protection. Under United States legislation, a cryptoasset qualifies as a security if it passes the Howey Test,[2] established by the Supreme Court in 1946. According to this test, an instrument is considered a security if it satisfies four criteria:

1. An investment of money: the investor commits capital or other assets to an enterprise.
2. In a common enterprise: the investment must be part of a common enterprise, whose outcomes depend on the efforts of others.
3. With the expectation of profit: investors must have a reasonable expectation of profit from their investment.
4. To be derived from the efforts of others: that profit or success must depend on the efforts or managerial decisions of third parties.

Under the European legislation, cryptoassets are considered financial instruments if they meet the definition of transferable securities provided by Article 4(1)(44) of

[2] Securities and Exchange Commission v. W. J. Howey Co., 328 U.S. 293 (1946)

MiFID II,[3] which defines them as "those classes of securities which are negotiable on the capital market, with the exception of instruments of payment" and include shares in companies, bonds and securitised debt, as well as "any other securities" giving: (i) a right to acquire or sell a transferable security; or (ii) giving rise to a cash settlement determined by reference to transferable securities, currencies, interest rates or yields, commodities or other indices or measures. This may include options, warrants, and structured bonds where the interest is linked to any derivative (e.g. selected stock index, interest rate, other derivate or a combination of derivatives). Therefore, similarly to the United States framework, European regulation requires that security cryptoassets exhibit the same substantive characteristics as traditional securities.

Security cryptoassets gained prominence following the ICO boom of 2017 and 2018, during which many offerings failed and prompted regulators to intervene. In this context of growing regulatory pressure and declining investor confidence, the idea emerged of creating an alternative mechanism that would preserve the technological advantages of blockchain while complying with existing legal frameworks. This gave rise to the Security Token Offering, or STO, which is a fundraising mechanism in which a cryptoasset is issued to the public in compliance with applicable securities regulation, meaning that issuers are required to meet disclosure obligations, investor protection standards and registration requirements with the relevant regulatory authorities. As a result, STOs offer investors a significantly higher degree of legal protection compared to unregulated ICOs, since the issued token grants the holder either cash flow rights linked to the project being financed or voting rights within the issuing organization, with such rights being legally enforceable under securities law.

The first documented STO dates back to 2017, when Blockchain Capital conducted what is considered the first offering structured as a security token, raising 10 million dollars through the BCAP token, which represented shares in its venture capital fund (Chavez-Dreyfuss, 2017). This pioneering experiment demonstrated the viability of the model, yet it was not until 2018 that the STO concept entered mainstream industry debate, precisely when the ICO market was collapsing. That same year, tZERO, a subsidiary of Overstock.com, conducted one of the most prominent STOs of the period, raising approximately 134 million dollars through a token structured as a security. The year 2018 was also when major regulatory authorities, most notably the SEC, began publishing specific guidance that effectively established the distinction between unregulated utility tokens and security tokens subject to securities laws.

Nevertheless, STOs remained an instrument that never fully gained traction, and in the more recent period the security cryptoasset market has shifted towards the tokenization of real-world assets. For instance, several fintech firms such as Ondo Finance have begun issuing tokens representing common stocks such as Apple and

[3] European Parliament and Council of the European Union. (2014). Directive 2014/65/EU on markets in financial instruments and amending Directive 2002/92/EC and Directive 2011/61/EU (MiFID II), Article 4(1)(44). Official Journal of the European Union, L 173, 349–496.

Tesla, backing each token on a one-to-one basis with the underlying asset and ensuring that the investor is exposed both to the capital gains of the traditional security and to its dividend income. These instruments are currently available only in certain jurisdictions and often restricted to professional investors, but broader access, including in Europe, is expected in the near future (Ondo Finance, 2025).

2.2.4 Stablecoin Cryptoassets

Stablecoins are cryptoassets whose value is pegged to the value of an underlying traditional asset, typically a fiat currency or commodity. The difference between this category and security cryptoassets lies in the fact that stablecoins do not confer participatory or ownership rights over an issuing entity, such as profit-sharing or voting rights. Stablecoins sometimes also show dramatic differences in terms of their legal, technical, functional and economic design. What these cryptoassets all have in common, however, is that their price stability cannot be equated with the stability of the assets they reference, as stablecoins introduce additional layers of risk such as counterparty risk or de-pegging risk, that are absent in the underlying reference assets.

Stablecoins usually reference fiat currencies such as the USD or EUR, but also commodities such as gold. They can be divided based on the mechanisms that guarantee the peg to the underlying asset. The peg can be guaranteed by a one-to-one collateralization of the underlying asset, with the collateral deposited at a third-party custodian institution. Alternatively, it can be maintained through a deposit of collateral represented by other cryptoassets, which often exceeds the value of the underlying asset in order to absorb potential losses in value due to market volatility. Finally, a third category of stablecoins stabilizes the value through an algorithm that, via smart contracts and expansions or contractions of the token supply, controls the price of the cryptoasset. Examples for these three categories are represented by Tether, DAI and TerraUSD respectively.

Tether Tether is today one of the most popular stablecoins, ranking 3rd by market capitalization at the end of December 2025 with nearly 160 billion dollars in value. Tether was launched in 2014 on Omni Layer, a secondary layer built on top of Bitcoin, but was later migrated to Ethereum as an ERC-20 token due to the slowness of transactions on the original infrastructure. Today, Ethereum and Tron host the highest volume of Tether transactions, as the stablecoin is deployed on both chains through the ERC-20 and TRC-20 smart contract standards respectively. This cryptoasset is pegged to the value of one US dollar through a one-to-one collateralization, with the collateral invested in highly liquid assets such as US Treasury Bills and similar instruments that back the circulating supply. Direct redemption from the issuer is available to customers who satisfy KYC procedures. This possibility ensures that the value of one Tether remains equal to one dollar through arbitrage. Indeed, when the market price of Tether falls below one dollar, arbitrageurs can purchase the cryptoasset on the open market and redeem it directly with the issuer, pocketing the positive differential. Conversely, when the value of Tether exceeds one dollar, they can purchase newly issued Tether directly from the issuer and sell it on the market, yielding the spread.

Dai DAI is a stablecoin pegged to the value of the US dollar with a market capitalization of over 4 billion dollars, ranking 22nd by market capitalization as of the end of December 2025. This cryptoasset is issued primarily on the Ethereum blockchain and on other blockchains. Its mechanism for stabilizing the value at one dollar is ensured through a system of overcollateralization with other cryptoassets. Specifically, through smart contracts denominated Maker Vaults, users can deposit cryptoassets and receive newly issued DAI in return as a debt position. The deposit must exceed the amount received in order to compensate for possible losses in value due to the volatility of the cryptoassets used as collateral. When the user wishes to recover the deposited collateral, it is sufficient to return to the protocol the quantity of DAI received, plus a fee denominated the Stability Fee. The returned DAI is automatically destroyed, reducing the circulating supply. Should the value of the collateral fall below the minimum required threshold, the protocol automatically liquidates the Vault, selling the deposited cryptoassets to repay the debt and guarantee the solvency of the entire system. The stabilization of the value is also ensured through an arbitrage mechanism. When DAI trades above one dollar, market participants have an incentive to open new Vaults, mint DAI at an implicit cost of one dollar and resell it on the market at a higher price, thereby increasing supply and pushing the price downward. Conversely, when DAI trades below one dollar, those with open Vaults have an incentive to repurchase DAI on the market at a discount to extinguish their debt, increasing demand and pushing the price upward.

TerraUSD TerraUSD (UST) was an algorithmic stablecoin pegged to the value of the US dollar, created in 2020 on the native Terra protocol and linked to the cryptoasset LUNA, which supported its stability. The stabilization mechanism was based on a system of direct arbitrage between UST and LUNA. The protocol guaranteed at all times the possibility of exchanging 1 UST for LUNA at a value equivalent to one dollar, and vice versa. When UST traded above one dollar, market participants had an incentive to purchase LUNA, convert it into UST through the protocol receiving tokens at a nominal value of one dollar, and resell UST on the market at a higher price, pocketing the difference. This process increased the supply of UST and reduced that of LUNA, pushing the price of UST downward until the peg was restored. Conversely, when UST traded below one dollar, it was convenient to purchase UST at a discount on the market and convert it into LUNA through the protocol, receiving a countervalue of one dollar, thereby increasing demand for UST and pushing its price upward. However, in May 2022, TerraUSD lost its peg to the US dollar and subsequently lost the entirety of its value. This was due to the critical vulnerability that TerraUSD depended entirely on confidence in the value of LUNA and on the continuity of demand for both cryptoassets. A series of massive sell-offs of UST triggered a devastating downward spiral, as the collapse in the price of UST pushed market participants to convert UST into LUNA in large quantities, dramatically increasing the supply of LUNA and causing its value to collapse. The depreciation of LUNA in turn undermined confidence in UST, generating further selling pressure in a self-reinforcing vicious cycle (Briola et al., 2023). Within a few days, UST lost its peg entirely and both cryptoassets fell from a combined market capitalization of approximately 55 billion dollars to just a few million.

2.2.5 Non-Fungible Token Cryptoassets

NFTs are cryptoassets representing ownership of unique digital or physical items and they are not mutually interchangeable, meaning that one NFT is not equivalent to another, as each token carries distinct attributes and provenance (Borri et al., 2022). The conceptual antecedents of NFTs can be traced back to the so-called "colored coins", an early experiment built on the Bitcoin blockchain that attempted to represent ownership of real-world assets by attaching metadata to small fractions of bitcoin. However, NFTs as they are known today emerged and gained traction following the introduction of the ERC-721 token standard, deployed on the Ethereum blockchain in 2018, which provided a standardized technical framework for the creation and management of non-fungible tokens. This cryptoasset category experienced remarkable growth between 2020 and 2021, driven by speculative demand and mainstream media attention, before collapsing in 2022, from which it has not significantly recovered. Two illustrative examples of NFT collections are CryptoKitties and Decentraland's LAND cryptoassets.

Cryptokitties CryptoKitties are NFTs representing unique digital cats, each characterized by a distinct combination of visual traits and attributes, referred to as "cattributes", generated through a pseudo-random algorithm at the time of minting. Launched in November 2017 by Dapper Labs on the Ethereum blockchain, CryptoKitties became one of the earliest demonstrations of the commercial viability of NFTs, attracting significant public attention and generating important transaction volumes. The collection's popularity was so pronounced that it caused considerable congestion on the Ethereum network, slowing transaction processing times and driving up gas fees across the entire platform (Jiang & Liu, 2021). An important feature of the CryptoKitties mechanics is the breeding system, through which two NFTs can be combined to produce a new token whose cattributes are algorithmically derived from those of the two parent tokens, introducing a gamification layer that incentivizes holding and trading. Scarcity plays a central role in the collection's value hierarchy, as the earliest generation cats, known as "Gen 0", were issued directly by the smart contract with a finite supply, making them significantly rarer and more valuable than later-generation tokens whose supply expands through user-driven breeding activity. In other words, the value of the collection can be understood as a product of investor psychology, in a manner not dissimilar to that observed in the traditional art market.

Land Decentraland is a decentralized virtual world built on the Ethereum blockchain, in which the constituent parcels of virtual land are represented as NFTs denominated as LAND cryptoassets. Each of these corresponds to a unique portion of virtual territory within the Decentraland map, conferring upon its holder the right to develop, monetize and govern the content displayed on that parcel, including interactive experiences, games and social spaces. The total supply of LAND is capped at approximately 90,000 parcels, a choice that introduces scarcity and underpins the asset's value proposition as digital real estate, since prices tend to rise as demand increases against a fixed supply. The platform operates through a dual-token economic model in which LAND governs ownership of virtual territory, while a separate fungible token, MANA, serves as the native currency of the ecosystem and is used to purchase LAND as well as virtual goods and services within the platform. From an economic standpoint, LAND cryptoassets attracted considerable speculative interest during the NFT market boom of 2021, with individual parcels selling at very high prices. The asset class also gained institutional traction, as major corporations established virtual presences within Decentraland. Samsung, for instance, acquired LAND to build a virtual store hosting product presentations and launch events (CNBC, 2022).

2.2.6 Utility Cryptoassets

The last category is that of utility cryptoassets. Following the definition provided by Lambert et al. (2022), utility cryptoassets are those that grant access to a community-based ecosystem by giving their holders a consumptive right on a product or service. This category encompasses all cryptoassets not included in the previous categories, functioning as a general class that captures the different functionalities and infrastructures of cryptoassets not covered elsewhere. In this category we find all those cryptoassets whose value is tied to the access they provide to a specific product or service, such as Basic Attention Token or Render. Additionally, this category includes cryptoassets that grant governance rights over a project, allowing holders to participate in strategic decisions or protocol modifications through a voting mechanism in which one cryptoasset corresponds to one vote. Such decisions may concern the rules of a crypto protocol or the direction of a decentralized organization, commonly referred to as a DAO. An example of a cryptoasset with such a function is Maker, which allows its holders to decide on modifications to the protocol that manages the operations of the DAI stablecoin.

Basic Attention Token Basic Attention Token is an ERC-20 token built on the Ethereum blockchain, launched in 2017 through one of the most successful initial coin offerings of that year, raising approximately 35 million dollars in under 30 seconds (CoinDesk, 2017). This cryptoasset is used within the ecosystem of Brave, a privacy-focused web browser that blocks any advertisement that is normally displayed on other web browsers such as Chrome or Firefox, guaranteeing users a better browsing experience. Users can decide whether to view advertisements in exchange for a payment for their attention in BAT, while advertisers who want to promote their products or services can purchase advertising space on the Brave browser by paying in BAT. The utility of this cryptoasset therefore lies in its capacity to monetize the attention of web users, something that does not occur in other browsers, while also guaranteeing advertisers access to a service, namely posting their advertisements on the network. As of the end of December 2025, it is ranked 121st by market capitalization.

Render Render is a cryptoasset that was originally launched on the Ethereum blockchain but has since migrated to the Solana blockchain. It gives holders access to the service of exploiting third-party GPUs to run the rendering of digital contents, which is the process that allows to obtain, starting from a 3D model, a highly realistic artificial image. In this way, even independent creators, by participating in the network, can produce high-quality 3D contents without having to purchase expensive hardware components, effectively democratizing access to computational resources. The Render Network is composed of hundreds of nodes that make their GPU available for this work. When a rendering job is submitted to the network, the workload is distributed across the nodes and the value of the job is calculated in terms of the cryptoasset, which will be paid by whoever rents the computational power and receives the finished product. The nodes that have made their GPU available receive Render as payment for their contribution. As of the end of December 2025, it is ranked 71st by market capitalization.

Maker Maker is an ERC-20 token built on the Ethereum blockchain, launched in 2017. This cryptoasset is the governance token of the MakerDAO protocol, which is the decentralized platform responsible for the issuance and management of the DAI stablecoin. Holders of Maker have the right to vote on key decisions regarding the protocol, such as the modification of the Stability Fee, the introduction of new types of accepted collateral and the risk parameters of the system. In this way, Maker holders act as the governing body of the protocol, making it one of the earliest and most prominent examples of decentralized governance in the DeFi ecosystem. Beyond governance, Maker also plays an important role in the stability mechanism of the protocol. In the event that the collateral backing DAI loses value too rapidly and the system incurs a deficit, new Maker tokens are minted and sold on the market to cover the shortfall, diluting existing holders. Conversely, when the system generates surplus revenue through the collection of Stability Fees, that surplus is used to buy back and burn Maker tokens, reducing the circulating supply, given that the maximum supply is fixed at 1 million Maker units. The utility of this cryptoasset therefore lies in granting holders governance rights over the protocol and also functioning as a recapitalization resource and value accrual mechanism for the ecosystem.

2.3 Conclusion

This chapter has provided a structured overview of the cryptoasset market, beginning with a clear definition and taxonomy of these instruments. The term "cryptoasset" has been adopted, following the terminology used by major regulatory bodies such as the European Securities and Markets Authority and the Financial Stability Board, as the most general identifier for any value exchanged digitally on a distributed ledger technology. A classification framework has subsequently been proposed based on the objective functionality that each cryptoasset serves, identifying six distinct categories, each characterized by a different value proposition and technical infrastructure: Payment, Infrastructure, Security, Stablecoins, NFT and Utility cryptoassets.

This classification is necessarily tentative, as the financial engineering industry and the broader crypto developer community continue to work on new types of cryptoassets whose characteristics may not fit neatly into the categories proposed here. Starting from Bitcoin in 2008, conceived as a simple peer-to-peer payment instrument, the cryptoasset ecosystem has evolved to encompass an increasingly wide range of economic and financial activities. This development suggests that further integration of blockchain technology with the real economy is not only possible but likely in the years ahead.

From an investment perspective, the key takeaway of this chapter is that not all cryptoassets are alike. Well-defined and functionally distinct categories exist, each with its own value drivers and risk characteristics. The investment decision remains subjective, depending on each investor's view of which technological developments will gain adoption and which categories of cryptoassets will consequently attract greater demand and therefore value.

References

Alonso, K. M., koe. (2018). *Zero to Monero: A technical guide to a private digital currency.* https://www.getmonero.org/es/library/Zero-to-Monero-1-0-0.pdf

Basel Committee on Banking Supervision. (2022). *Prudential treatment of cryptoasset exposures.* Bank for International Settlements.

Borri, N., Liu, Y., & Tsyvinski, A. (2022). The economics of non-fungible tokens. *SSRN Journal.* https://doi.org/10.2139/ssrn.4052045

Briola, A., Vidal-Tomás, D., Wang, Y., & Aste, T. (2023). Anatomy of a Stablecoin's failure: The Terra-Luna case. *Finance Research Letters, 51*, 103358. https://doi.org/10.1016/j.frl.2022.103358

Chavez-Dreyfuss, G. (2017). *U.S. venture capital firm raises $10 million in six-hour token sale.* Reuters. https://www.reuters.com/article/technology/us-venture-capital-firm-raises-10-million-in-six-hour-token-sale-idUSKBN17M231/

CNBC. (2022). *Samsung held an event in the metaverse and it didn't quite go to plan.* https://www.cnbc.com/2022/02/10/samsung-held-an-event-in-the-metaverse-and-it-didnt-quite-go-to-plan.html

CoinDesk. (2017). *$35 million in 30 seconds: Token sale for internet browser brave sells out.* https://www.coindesk.com/markets/2017/05/31/35-million-in-30-seconds-token-sale-for-internet-browser-brave-sells-out?utm_source=chatgpt.com

Eska, F. E., Shi, Y., Theissen, E., & Uhrig-Homburg, M. (2025). Design and valuation of cryptocurrencies. *Review of Quantitative Finance and Accounting*. https://doi.org/10.1007/s11156-025-01447-9

European Union. (2023). *Regulation (EU) 2023/1114 of the European parliament and of the council of 31 May 2023 on markets in crypto-assets.*

Freni, P., Ferro, E., & Moncada, R. (2022). Tokenomics and blockchain tokens: A design-oriented morphological framework. *Blockchain: Research and Applications, 3*, 100069. https://doi.org/10.1016/j.bcra.2022.100069

Fry, J., & Ibiloye, O. (2023). Towards a taxonomy for crypto assets. *Cogent Economics & Finance, 11*, 2207266. https://doi.org/10.1080/23322039.2023.2207266

Härdle, W. K., Harvey, C. R., & Reule, R. C. G. (2020). Understanding cryptocurrencies. *Journal of Financial Econometrics, 18*, 181–208. https://doi.org/10.1093/jjfinec/nbz033

Jiang, X.-J., & Liu, X. F. (2021). CryptoKitties transaction network analysis: The rise and fall of the first blockchain game mania. *Frontiers in Physics, 9*, 631665. https://doi.org/10.3389/fphy.2021.631665

Lambert, T., Liebau, D., & Roosenboom, P. (2022). Security token offerings. Small. *Business Economics, 59*, 299–325. https://doi.org/10.1007/s11187-021-00539-9

Ondo Finance. (2025). *Ondo secures EU regulatory approval for tokenized stocks and ETFs.* https://ondo.finance/blog/ondo-eu-regulatory-approval

Spurr, A., & Ausloos, M. (2021). Challenging practical features of bitcoin by the main altcoins. *Quality and Quantity, 55*, 1541–1559. https://doi.org/10.1007/s11135-020-01062-x

Thakur, Y. (2025). *How Solana achieves lightning-fast transactions.* Medium. URL https://medium.com/@sincerelyyyash/how-solana-achieves-lightning-fast-transactions-ee02e79d7eb4

Chapter 3
Cryptocurrencies as a Financial Asset: A Bibliometric Review

3.1 Introduction

Since the creation of Bitcoin in 2008, scholars and practitioners have sought to understand what cryptocurrencies are and what value they serve in real-world applications. Over time, the perception of cryptocurrencies has evolved considerably, initially being considered as currencies (Dyhrberg, 2016), then speculative assets (Fry & Cheah, 2016) and later as investment assets (Kuo Chuen et al., 2017), at least among those who believe that blockchain technology holds significant promise for the future. Considerable uncertainty, however, still persists. Some studies classify cryptocurrencies as commodities akin to gold (Kyriazis, 2020), on account of their store-of-value function, while others challenge this view (Klein et al., 2018). Furthermore, an active debate continues regarding the role of cryptocurrencies in investors' portfolios, both as instruments of diversification (Goodell & Goutte, 2021; Somoza & Didisheim, 2022; Wang et al., 2025) and as hedge and safe haven assets, that is, assets providing protection during periods of market stress (Baur et al., 2022; Bouri et al., 2017; Liu & Yuan, 2024; Wang et al., 2019). The aim of this study is therefore to review the literature examining the economic and financial dimensions of cryptocurrencies, with a view to offering scholars and practitioners a more comprehensive picture of the state of the art in research on cryptocurrencies as a financial asset and distinct asset class.

The chaotic nature of the surrounding literature, coupled with the absence of a systematic review specifically addressing this aspect, justifies the need to map and study this research area. Prior reviews are few, often outdated, and focus predominantly on general aspects of cryptocurrencies, without exploring in depth the understanding of cryptocurrencies as a financial asset class and their role in investors' portfolios (Corbet et al., 2019; Jalal et al., 2025).

D. Sandretto, *Cryptocurrencies as an Asset Class*, SpringerBriefs in Finance,
https://doi.org/10.1007/978-3-032-31491-8_3

To address this gap, the present study combines bibliometric and content analysis to map and interpret the latest trends in the literature, guided by three research questions:

RQ1: What are the most impactful articles in this field?
RQ2: What are the most influential journals and authors?
RQ3: What are the intellectual structure and research streams in the literature?

To this end, a bibliometric analysis is performed adhering to the SPAR-4-SLR research protocol (Paul et al., 2021), which ensures the reliability and replicability of the research findings, and is consistent with established methodological approaches in the field (Donthu et al., 2021; Mukherjee et al., 2022).

The data consist of 1490 articles retrieved from the Web of Science database, spanning the period from 2014 to 2025. Only documents classified under the Economics and Business Finance categories and written in English are retained (Jalal et al., 2025). The analysis is conducted using Bibliometrix (Aria & Cuccurullo, 2017), RStudio and VOSviewer (van Eck & Waltman, 2010), through which a performance analysis and science mapping exercise is carried out (Donthu et al., 2021; Lal et al., 2022) to address each of the research questions in turn.

This study contributes to the literature by conducting a systematic and comprehensive review of the role of cryptocurrencies as financial assets. A holistic assessment of the field is provided by identifying the most influential authors and journals and by mapping the structure and content of its research streams, thereby enabling scholars and individuals interested in the topic to develop a thorough and accessible understanding of this research area. The findings are of interest to academics, as they summarize the state of the recent literature and offer guidance for future research, helping scholars to advance the field and avoid stagnation. The implications equally extend to practitioners, who may benefit by gaining a clearer framework for positioning this emerging asset class within their investment strategies.

3.2 Data and Methodology

Bibliometric analysis is a quantitative methodology extensively used to assess large volumes of published research through the application of statistical tools, reducing the interpretation biases typically associated with qualitative reviews driven by authors' backgrounds (Pandey et al., 2023). This technique allows for the examination of the intellectual structure of a specific domain within the extant literature (Donthu et al., 2021). In particular, it makes possible to analyze trends, citations, and co-citations of a particular theme across various dimensions such as year, country, author, journal, method, theory, and research problem (Paul & Criado, 2020). Given these properties, bibliometric analyses have been widely adopted across disciplines to summarize the state of the art of a given field, including economics (Andolšek et al., 2026; Zhu et al., 2019), finance (Chiaramonte et al., 2023; Sandretto et al., 2026) and management (Budler et al., 2021; Ramos-Rodríguez & Ruíz-Navarro, 2004).

In light of the popularity and objectivity of this method, bibliometric analysis is employed here to review the literature on the analysis of cryptocurrencies as a financial asset and as a new asset class. To ensure reliability, replicability, and minimal bias in research findings, the SPAR-4-SLR research protocol is adopted (Paul et al., 2021). Additionally, the methodology proposed by Donthu et al. (2021) to identify research clusters is followed, encompassing two primary techniques: performance analysis, which focuses on evaluating the contributions of research constituents to a given field (Cobo et al., 2011; Ramos-Rodríguez & Ruíz-Navarro, 2004), and science mapping, which refers to the examination of relationships between such constituents (Baker et al., 2021; Cobo et al., 2011). The mixed approach employed in this investigation is illustrated in Fig. 3.1.

Following the SPAR-4-SLR research protocol, papers and bibliographic data are collected from Web of Science (WoS), covering the period from 31 October 2008 (the publication date of the Bitcoin whitepaper) to 31 December 2025. WoS represents the standard database choice for bibliometric studies, given its high quality (Khan et al., 2022) and its status as the most widely used tool for generating bibliometric data, encompassing around 34,000 journals (Birkle et al., 2020; Korom, 2019).

To identify articles related to the research domain, a search string is developed comprising keywords coherent with the topic of investigation and already adopted in previous bibliometric analyses (Jalal et al., 2025), such as "Bitcoin", "Cryptocurrency", and "asset class". Specifically, the search string is as follows: TS = ((Bitcoin OR Cryptocurrenc*) AND ("financial asset" OR "financial assets" OR "asset" OR "assets" OR "asset class")). After retrieving the articles, keywords are further validated through cross-referencing with highly cited papers.

A search using these keywords leads to an initial sample of 3161 papers. The documents are then filtered to include only articles written in English and belonging to the Business Finance and Economics categories, consistently with the approach of Jalal et al. (2025). Notably, no filters based on journal quality rankings such as ABS or ABDC are imposed, as doing so could introduce sample bias and compromise a correct assessment and mapping of the literature.

Applying the above-mentioned filters results in a sample of 1494 articles. A further 4 studies are subsequently removed as they are marked as retracted, yielding a final sample of 1490 articles. Bibliometric analysis is performed using the bibliometrix package (Aria & Cuccurullo, 2017) and VOSviewer visualization software (van Eck & Waltman, 2010). Table 3.1 summarizes the main descriptive statistics of the final sample. The 1490 articles are published across 283 journals and co-authored by 2900 scholars, with an average of 3 authors per article and 23 citations per paper. Notably, the earliest articles in the sample date back to 2014, suggesting that academic interest in cryptocurrencies as financial assets emerged only several years after the creation of Bitcoin.

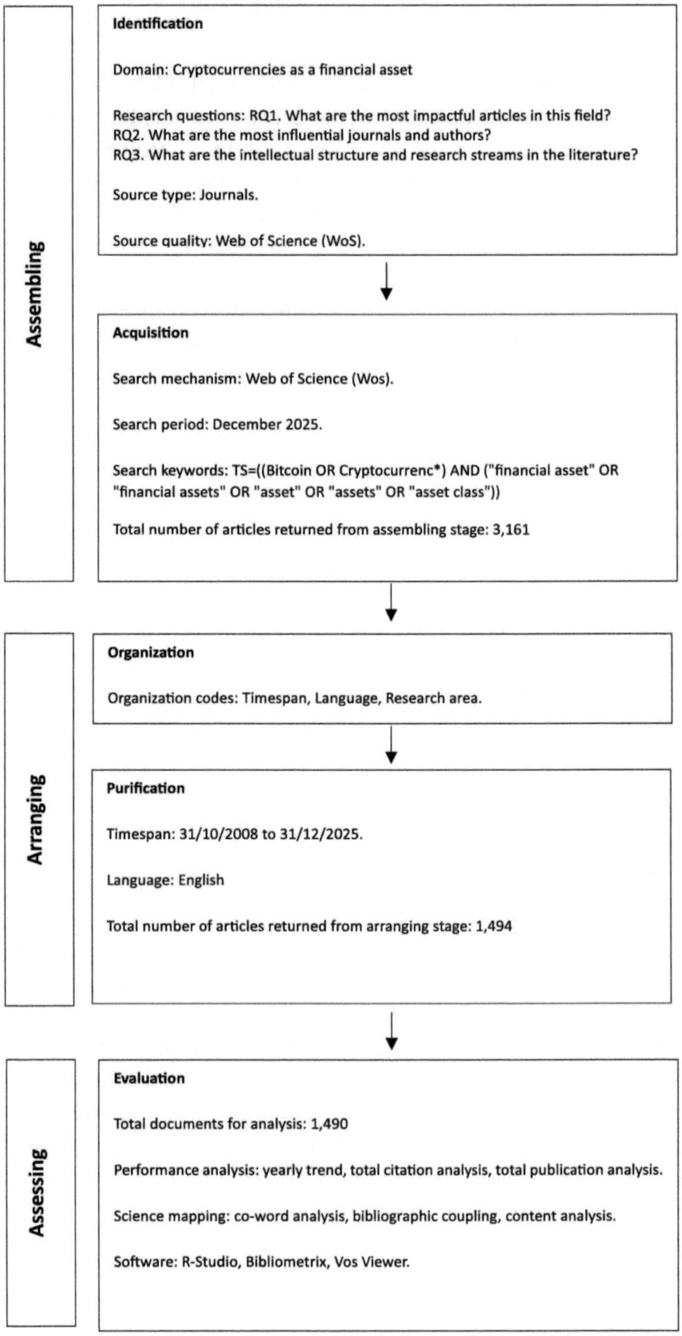

Fig. 3.1 SPAR-4-SLR protocol Source: Author's elaboration on Paul et al. (2021)

Table 3.1 Main information about data

Description	Results
Timespan	2014:2025
N. Of journals	283
Articles	1490
Annual growth rate %	23.01
Document average age	3.1
Average citations per doc	23.57
References	34,727
Keywords plus	1004
Author's keywords	3294
Authors	2900
Single-authored docs	208
Co-authors per doc	2.79
International co-authorships %	39.93

Source: Author's elaboration using Bibliometrix

3.3 Results

Following the guidelines provided by Donthu et al. (2021), the first step of the analysis consists of a performance investigation aimed at examining the publication trend of the collected articles. Specifically, the total number of publications over time is evaluated across variables such as year, authorship, journal, and affiliated organizations. As a second step, a comprehensive science mapping is performed through co-word analysis, bibliographic coupling, and content analysis, in order to identify and trace the different research themes emerging from the literature on cryptocurrencies as a financial asset and as a new asset class.

3.3.1 Performance Analysis

Figure 3.2 illustrates the distribution of articles over time. In the early years, the number of publications on this theme was limited, but subsequently grew exponentially. Strikingly, in 2024 the number of published studies exceeded 250, with the curve showing an even steeper increase in 2025, reaching over 350 articles. This trend speaks to the scientific community's growing interest in cryptocurrencies and confirms an increasing tendency to regard them as financial assets.

Considering the sources of the articles, there are 283 different journals in which the papers are published. Table 3.2 provides an overview of the top 20 most prolific journals in this domain, ranked by total number of publications along with their associated source quality indicators. It stands out that the journal that published the most articles in this domain is *Finance Research Letters*, with a total of 139 articles,

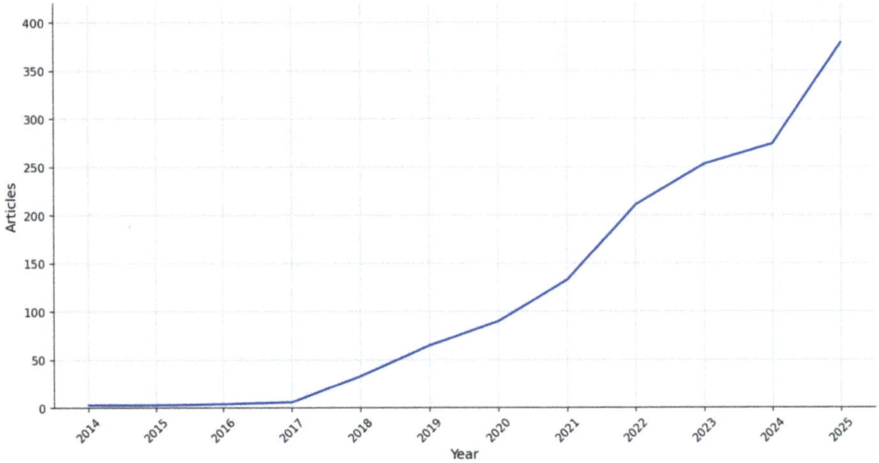

Fig. 3.2 Annual scientific production of articles. Source: Author's elaboration using Bibliometrix

followed by other Elsevier journals such as *Research in International Business and Finance* with 78, *International Review of Financial Analysis* with 73, *North American Journal of Economics and Finance* with 53, and *Financial Innovation* with 44. Looking at the dynamic evolution of the cumulative distribution of articles published in the most prolific journals in Fig. 3.3, it is again possible to observe that *Finance Research Letters* is a consistent outlet where the largest number of works on this topic are published over time. These are therefore the journals that researchers or individuals interested in the topic should consult to deepen their understanding of the subject.

Moving now to authors and article performance measures, Table 3.3 reports the most influential authors based on local citations, which indicate the popularity of articles within the network of 1490 publications. This analysis is particularly interesting for individuals who want to know who the leading authors in the field are, and for researchers seeking to identify potential future collaborations (Migliavacca et al., 2022). It stands out that the most cited works are those of E. Bouri from the Lebanese American University, L. Yarovaya from the University of Southampton, and B. Lucey from Trinity College Dublin, with 576, 568, and 564 local citations respectively. The results also show that the top 10 leading scholars in this field of research come from different institutions across the globe, indicating a good diversification of influential scholars across countries, in contrast to the traditional dominance of US scholars in finance research.

As the influence of the articles is measured in terms of citations (Pandey et al., 2023), Table 3.4 displays the 5 most influential articles, ranked by global citations, i.e. the number of times each article has been referenced within WoS. The paper that has received the highest number of citations (937) is the seminal work by Dyhrberg (2016). The author investigates whether Bitcoin has properties more similar to the US Dollar or Gold, analyzing their variance processes by means of GARCH

Table 3.2 Most productive journals

Rank	Journal	# articles	Publisher	ABS ranking	ABDC ranking	SJR
1	*Finance research letters*	139	Elsevier	2	A	1.711
2	*Research in international business and finance*	78	Elsevier	2	A	1.415
3	*International review of financial analysis*	73	Elsevier	3	A	2.288
4	*North American journal of economics and finance*	53	Elsevier	2	B	0.961
5	*Financial innovation*	44	Springer nature	2	B	1.287
6	*International review of economics and finance*	44	Elsevier	2	A	1.372
7	*Computational economics*	42	Springer nature	1	B	0.535
8	*Applied economics*	33	Taylor & Francis	2	A	0.616
9	*Applied economics letters*	33	Taylor & Francis	1	B	0.384
10	*Journal of international financial markets, institutions and money*	33	Elsevier	3	A	1.522
11	*Journal of risk and financial management*	30	MPDI	–	–	0.480
12	*Studies in economics and finance*	29	Emerald	1	B	0.457
13	*Economics letters*	28	Elsevier	3	A	0.755
14	*Risks*	26	MPDI	–	–	0.397
15	*Cogent economics and finance*	21	Taylor & Francis	1	B	0.539
16	*Energy economics*	19	Elsevier	3	A*	3.919
17	*Quarterly review of economics and finance*	18	Elsevier	2	B	0.725
18	*Journal of risk finance*	17	Emerald	1	B	0.821
19	*Financial and credit activity-problems of theory and practice*	16	Fintech Aliance	–	–	0.201
20	*International journal of finance and economics*	16	Wiley-Blackwell	3	B	0.791

Note: The ABS ranking refers to the journal quality guide developed by the Chartered Association of Business Schools (CABS), where journals are ranked from 4* (highest) to 1 (lowest). Source: https://charteredabs.org/academic-journal-guide. The ABDC ranking refers to the journal quality list compiled by the Australian Business Deans Council (ABDC), where journals are classified into four tiers: A* (highest), A, B, and C (lowest). Source: https://abdc.edu.au/abdc-journal-quality-list. The SJR (SCImago Journal Rank) measures journal impact by accounting for both the number of citations received by a journal and the prestige of the citing journals. Source: https://www.scimagojr.com/journalrank.php. Source: Author's elaboration using Bibliometrix

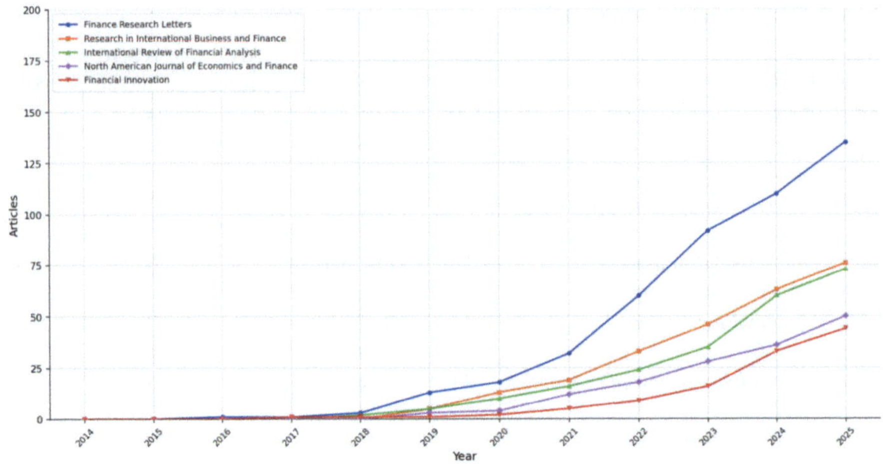

Fig. 3.3 Most productive journals over time. Source: Author's elaboration using Bibliometrix

Table 3.3 Most influential authors

Rank	Author	Local Citations	Articles	Affiliation	Country
1	Bouri, Elie	576	24	Lebanese American University	Lebanon
2	Yarovaya, Larisa	568	18	University of Southampton	UK
3	Lucey, Brian	564	11	Trinity College Dublin	Ireland
4	Corbet, Shaen	502	19	Dublin City University	Ireland
5	Roubaud, David	386	8	Montpellier Business School	France
6	Larkin, Charles	379	6	University of Bath	UK
7	Baur, Dirk	378	5	University of Western Australia	Australia
8	Dyhrberg, Anne Haubo	307	2	University of Delaware	USA
9	Meegan, Andrew	306	3	Dublin City University	Ireland
10	Mensi, Walid	286	14	Sultan Qaboos University	Oman

Source: Author's elaboration using Bibliometrix

models. She found that Bitcoin exhibits both medium of exchange and store of value variance behaviors, which categorize it as a new financial asset useful for portfolio management. Corbet et al. (2018), cited 908 times, undertake a more comprehensive analysis, examining the volatility connectedness between cryptocurrencies and other financial assets. The authors conclude that the cryptocurrency market represents a new investment asset class, since cryptocurrencies are relatively isolated from market shocks and decoupled from traditional financial assets. The third most cited study is Cheah and Fry (2015), which provides evidence that Bitcoin is a speculative financial asset, as it exhibits a high bubble component in its pricing and a null fundamental value. Finally, the fourth study by Baur et al. (2018), by

Table 3.4 Top 5 most influential articles

Authors	Title	Journal	Year	Total citation	Citation per year
Dyhrberg A. H.	Bitcoin, gold and the dollar—A GARCH volatility analysis	*Finance research letters*	2016	937	85.18
Corbet S. et al.	Exploring the dynamic relationships between cryptocurrencies and other financial assets	*Economics letters*	2018	908	100.89
Cheat E., Fry J.	Speculative bubbles in bitcoin markets? An empirical investigation into the fundamental value of bitcoin	*Economics letters*	2015	843	70.25
Baur D. et al.	Bitcoin: Medium of exchange or speculative assets?	*Journal of international financial markets, institutions and money*	2018	815	90.56
Klein T. et al.	Bitcoin is not the new gold—A comparison of volatility, correlation, and portfolio performance	*International review of financial analysis*	2018	520	57.78

Source: Author's elaboration using Bibliometrix

analyzing the Bitcoin public ledger, documents that it is not used as a medium of exchange but rather as a speculative asset, whereas Klein et al. (2018) debunk the myth that Bitcoin can be considered digital gold, showing that it behaves differently from it.

Overall, the highest cited papers all investigate what function cryptocurrencies — and especially Bitcoin as the reference coin — serve, and whether they share the similar characteristics with other financial assets. Their findings converge on the conclusion that cryptocurrencies represent a new asset class, both from an econometric and a practical standpoint.

3.3.2 *Science Mapping*

Science mapping analyses the interrelationships and structural connections among research elements to understand the intellectual interactions within a field (Donthu et al., 2021). The study continues by charting the intellectual structure of the literature by conducting bibliographic coupling, content analysis and co-word analysis using the VOSViewer visualization software (van Eck & Waltman, 2010).

The main thematic clusters are identified by means of bibliographic coupling. This method for scientific mapping assumes that two papers sharing equal references will also have similar content (Kessler, 1963; Weinberg, 1974). Unlike co-citation analysis, which prioritizes highly cited publications and excludes recent or niche publications from thematic clusters, bibliographic coupling is more suitable for scholars seeking to uncover a wide range of themes and their latest developments, providing a representation of the current state of the research field (Donthu et al., 2021).

Based on Fig. 3.4, out of a total of 1490 documents, 169 meet the minimum threshold of 50 citations (Sandretto et al., 2026). The outcome of this analysis is the identification of four main thematic clusters, with the largest comprising 79 items.

As a consequent step, content analysis is employed to study and classify the clusters. This approach involves examining the most influential and linked articles within each cluster, a standard practice in bibliometric literature (Baker et al., 2021; Boubaker et al., 2023).

Bitcoin The red cluster in Fig. 3.4 includes 79 articles that investigate the properties and role of Bitcoin as a financial asset. Not surprisingly, Bitcoin, as the most popular and highly capitalized cryptocurrency, has attracted considerable research attention.

Within this research stream falls the highly influential paper by Dyhrberg (2016). In this article, the author found that Bitcoin's variance shares similar features with the US dollar and gold, positioning it as an hybrid asset that serves both as a medium of exchange and a store of value. In contrast, the more comprehensive work by Klein et al. (2018) provided evidence that Bitcoin cannot be regarded as digital gold. More specifically, the authors found that Bitcoin behaves fundamentally differently from gold, particularly during market turmoils, where Bitcoin does not exhibit the safe-haven or hedging properties that gold offers for traditional investments.

A number of papers have devoted efforts to analyzing Bitcoin as a portfolio diversifier. Platanakis and Urquhart (2020) investigated the potential out-of-sample benefits of adding Bitcoin to a stock-bond portfolio across a variety of asset allocation strategies, finding that it improves portfolio risk-return ratios. Similar

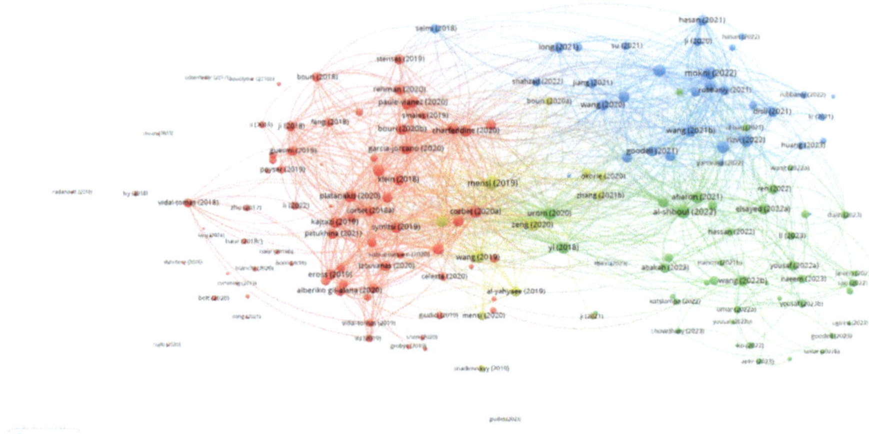

Fig. 3.4 Bibliographic coupling analysis network. Source: Author's elaboration using Bibliometrix

conclusions are drawn from the study by Symitsi and Chalvatzis (2019), who identified Bitcoin as an effective portfolio diversifier. Further evidence on a global basis is documented by Kajtazi and Moro (2019), who analyzed the diversification properties of Bitcoin within a portfolio of US, European and Chinese assets, documenting an overall improvement in the risk-return trade-off.

Closely related, other studies have explored the spillover effects and tail dependencies of Bitcoin with other assets. Ji et al. (2018) analyzed the contemporaneous and lagged relations between Bitcoin and other asset classes during the period 2010 to 2017, documenting that Bitcoin exhibits relatively independent price behavior in specific periods, though with lower diversification benefits during Bitcoin bear markets. Using the same sample period, Bouri et al. (2018) analyzed volatility spillovers between Bitcoin and traditional assets, finding that the cryptocurrency market is not completely isolated, as Bitcoin is affected by volatility originating from other markets, particularly during market downturns. Smales (2019) investigated the safe-haven properties of Bitcoin, highlighting that it does not act as a safe haven but only as a weak hedge. The author further questioned the effectiveness of Bitcoin as a safe haven given its high volatility during periods of market distress, which reduces liquidity and increases transaction costs in terms of both time and fees, rendering it an unsuitable safe-haven asset beforehand. Corbet et al. (2020) further stressed that Bitcoin is not a useful diversifier, with important implications for diversification benefits and safe-haven properties, analyzing a more recent period.

Overall, it can be summarized that Bitcoin differs substantially from gold, failing to provide the hedging or safe-haven properties that gold exhibits during market turmoil, while standing out as a diversifier under normal market conditions.

Spillovers and Connectedness The green cluster comprises 43 research articles associated with return and volatility spillovers and the connectedness between cryptocurrencies and other financial assets.

On one hand, a number of studies focus on general spillovers between cryptocurrencies and traditional asset classes. For instance, Ugolini et al. (2023) investigated return spillovers between DeFi cryptoassets, cryptocurrencies, equities and safe-haven assets, finding that all asset classes are influenced primarily by their own shocks, while spillovers between DeFi cryptos and other cryptocurrencies are the most pronounced. The connectedness between markets is shown to be time-varying and intensified during the pandemic. Elsayed et al. (2022) provided evidence that policy uncertainty in cryptocurrency markets affects other uncertainty measures, and further find that gold acts as a net receiver of both return and volatility spillovers under bearish, bullish and normal market conditions, making it highly sensitive to uncertainty shocks and significantly affected by cryptocurrency markets. Interestingly, Yousaf et al. (2023) investigated whether meme coins can significantly destabilize financial markets during periods of speculative euphoria, showing that meme stocks and meme tokens exhibit time-varying connectedness with traditional financial assets.

On the other hand, part of the literature has concentrated on the NFT market. Wang (2022) constructed an NFT attention index based on 590 million news items and used it to estimate volatility spillover connectedness between NFT markets and other financial markets, concluding that NFT markets exhibit a relatively independent and isolated character compared to other financial markets and cryptocurrencies. These weak connections are also confirmed by Yousaf and Yarovaya (2022). Differently, Umar et al. (2022) provided evidence that return and volatility spillovers among these markets increased during the pandemic. Finally, some studies address the sustainability dimension of cryptocurrencies and its implications for risk spillovers. For instance, Duan et al. (2023) compared clean and dirty cryptocurrencies against traditional and green assets using a TVP-VAR framework for dynamic connectedness, finding that cryptocurrencies generally transmit limited information to financial assets, but that clean cryptocurrencies are even less connected than the dirty group, particularly in the post-pandemic period.

Overall, the literature suggests that cryptocurrency spillovers occur primarily within the crypto market itself, though in certain circumstances such as severe market downturns, these can extend to and influence traditional financial markets.

Covid-19 The blue cluster comprises 34 research papers linked to the analysis of cryptocurrency behavior during the Covid-19 pandemic.

In the wake of the Covid-19 market downturn, scholars seized the opportunity to further study the safe-haven properties of cryptocurrencies — defined, following Baur and Lucey (2010), as assets exhibiting negative correlation with other assets during periods of market stress.

Studies by Disli et al. (2021), Mokni et al. (2022) and Ji et al. (2020) indicated that cryptocurrencies did not act as safe-haven assets during the financial turbulence of the pandemic period. However, as pointed out by Rubbaniy et al. (2021), when a non-financial measure of market distress is employed — such as the fear sentiment of households and retail investors — cryptocurrencies do appear to act as safe havens. Chemkha et al. (2021) argued that Bitcoin did not function as a safe haven during the pandemic in the manner that gold did, yet its ability to hedge other asset classes remained present, reflected in a near-zero correlation with other assets. Differently, Goodell and Goutte (2021) documented that Bitcoin, Litecoin and Ethereum did not act as safe havens even with respect to the equity market, while the stablecoin Tether did act as a safe-haven asset for equities.

Lastly, some articles address the general effect of the Covid-19 shock on the cryptocurrency market. Yarovaya et al. (2022) analyzed the consequences of the pandemic shock on the cryptocurrency market, highlighting how cryptocurrencies experienced severe drawdowns exceeding 50%, while also exhibiting the highest reactivity and recovery rates among the financial assets studied. However, not all cryptocurrencies reacted in the same manner. Iqbal et al. (2021), studying the market returns of 10 cryptocurrencies in relation to varying levels of Covid-19 intensity, found an asymmetric reaction on an individual rather than average basis, with Bitcoin, Ethereum, Cardano and Cronos performing better compared to the other currencies.

In sum, these studies highlight that Covid-19 represented a structural break that challenged prevailing assumptions about the behavior of cryptocurrencies relative to traditional markets. The mixed results found across studies may stem from differing methodological choices and the variety of cryptocurrencies analyzed.

Commodity and Cryptocurrencies The last cluster, shown in yellow, is the smallest with 13 articles and consists of research investigating the correlations and interdependencies between cryptocurrencies and commodities, given that cryptocurrencies have also been considered as a potential commodity in their own right (Gronwald, 2019).

Mensi et al. (2019) showed that Bitcoin is significantly connected with precious metals such as gold, silver, palladium and platinum, although it tends to function more as a receiver than a driver of volatility spillovers. Al-Yahyaee et al. (2019) instead compared Bitcoin and gold in portfolios exposed to oil and the S&P GSCI, finding that both assets provide diversification and hedging benefits, even if gold preserves a more stable protective role. Focusing specifically on energy markets, Okorie and Lin (2020) found that the relationship between crude oil and cryptocurrencies is not uniform, as the direction and intensity of volatility spillovers vary across individual coins. Finally, Ji et al. (2019) broadened the perspective by showing that cryptocurrencies are embedded in the wider commodity network, although agricultural and energy commodities remain the core nodes of that system. Overall, this cluster suggests that cryptocurrencies are linked to commodity markets through multiple transmission channels. Nonetheless, their function rests more conditional and less stable than that of traditional commodities such as gold.

As a further analytical step, the most frequently used keywords are identified to confirm whether the research streams uncovered are consistent with the written content of the publications (Emich et al., 2020; Lal et al., 2022). Co-word analysis operates under the assumption that words commonly occurring together share a thematic connection. Figure 3.5 depicts the 62 keywords meeting the threshold of a minimum of 30 occurrences. The red cluster connects "bitcoin" with "volatility", "returns", "dynamics", "inefficiency" and "risk", emphasizing and confirming the cluster concerned with the investigation of the properties and role of Bitcoin as a financial asset. The blue cluster instead connects words such as "hedge", "safe haven" and "diversification", linking this thematic cluster to the findings of the previous analysis when considering the impact of Covid-19. Even though the word "covid-19" pertains to the green cluster, it appears in close proximity to the blue one and is not included within it simply because co-word analysis, unlike bibliographic coupling, groups research streams by thematic occurrence rather than citations (Klarin, 2024). Finally, the green cluster gathers themes relating to spillovers and connectedness among cryptocurrencies, with keywords such as "spillovers", "connectedness", "dependence" and "contagion", but also incorporates the cluster focusing on commodities and oil, given the presence of words such as "commodities" and "crude oil". This is again a consequence of co-word analysis, which groups keywords by co-occurrence rather than citations.

Nevertheless, the main topics identified qualitatively correspond to those uncovered in the previous content analysis, confirming the robustness of the investigation (Patel et al., 2022).

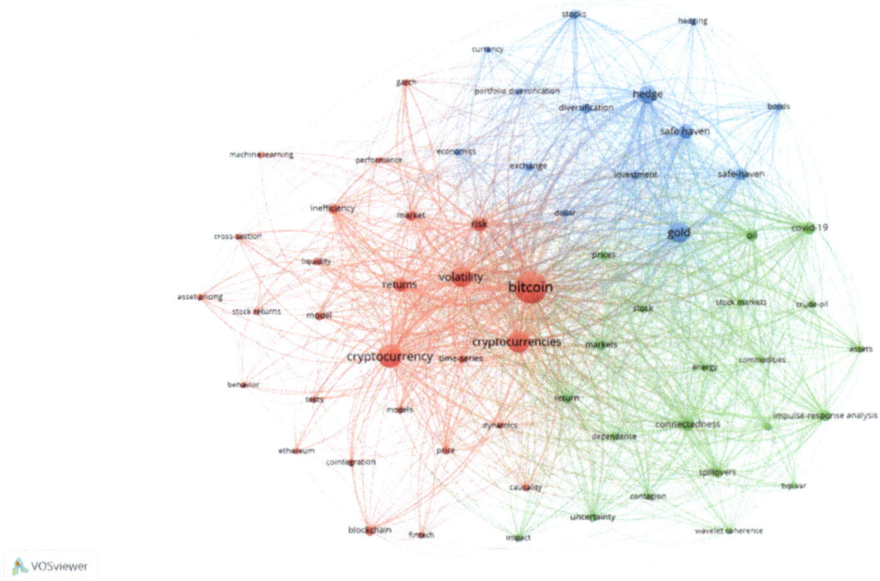

Fig. 3.5 Co-word analysis network. Source: Author's elaboration using Bibliometrix

3.4 Conclusion

This chapter conducts a bibliometric and content analysis of the literature on cryptocurrencies as a financial asset, covering the period from the creation of Bitcoin through to the end of December 2025. A total of 1490 articles published in finance and economics journals are examined to identify the most influential articles, authors and journals, as well as the prevailing research themes in this domain. The analysis adheres to the SPAR-4-SLR research protocol (Paul et al., 2021), which is designed to uphold the reliability and replicability of research findings, and employs the two bibliometric methods proposed by Donthu et al. (2021), namely performance analysis and science mapping.

The results show that the most influential articles and authors on this topic are geographically well distributed, while Finance Research Letters, with 139 publications, emerges as the leading outlet in the field. Through a combination of co-word analysis, bibliographic coupling and content analysis, four research streams are identified. The first concerns the properties and role of Bitcoin as a financial asset, with the evidence suggesting that it can serve as an effective diversifier, but falls short of providing the hedging and safe haven properties associated with gold. The second stream addresses spillovers and connectedness among cryptocurrencies, with the literature indicating that such spillovers occur predominantly within the crypto market itself, though they can spill over into traditional financial markets under conditions of severe market stress. The third stream regards Covid-19 as a structural break that altered the correlation structure between cryptocurrencies and traditional assets. The fourth and smallest stream explores the nexus between commodities and cryptocurrencies, finding that while cryptocurrencies are connected to commodity markets, their role remains marginal.

These findings offer academics a clearer orientation toward the central open questions in this field, helping to avoid unnecessary duplication of effort and directing attention toward areas that warrant further investigation. The results are equally relevant to practitioners and investment professionals seeking to better understand how cryptocurrencies can be integrated into portfolio construction strategies.

Finally, the study is subject to a number of limitations that may open avenues for future research. The analysis is restricted to articles indexed in Web of Science, and the search string employed may not have captured the full breadth of relevant work given the vastness of this research area. Future studies may therefore benefit from adopting a broader and more exhaustive search strategy across multiple databases.

References

Al-Yahyaee, K. H., Mensi, W., Al-Jarrah, I. M. W., Hamdi, A., & Kang, S. H. (2019). Volatility forecasting, downside risk, and diversification benefits of bitcoin and oil and international commodity markets: A comparative analysis with yellow metal. *The North American Journal of Economics and Finance, 49*, 104–120. https://doi.org/10.1016/j.najef.2019.04.001

Andolšek, J., Černe, M., & Lamovšek, A. (2026). Mapping the milestones of modern times: Intellectual landscape of political economy through bibliometric analysis. *Journal of Economic Surveys, 40*, 821–838. https://doi.org/10.1111/joes.70023

Aria, M., & Cuccurullo, C. (2017). Bibliometrix: An R-tool for comprehensive science mapping analysis. *Journal of Informetrics, 11*, 959–975. https://doi.org/10.1016/j.joi.2017.08.007

Baker, H. K., Kumar, S., & Pandey, N. (2021). Forty years of the journal of futures markets: A bibliometric overview. *Journal of Futures Markets, 41*, 1027–1054. https://doi.org/10.1002/fut.22211

Baur, D. G., Hoang, L. T., & Hossain, M. Z. (2022). Is bitcoin a hedge? How extreme volatility can destroy the hedge property. *Finance Research Letters, 47*, 102655. https://doi.org/10.1016/j.frl.2021.102655

Baur, D. G., Hong, K., & Lee, A. D. (2018). Bitcoin: Medium of exchange or speculative assets? *Journal of International Financial Markets, Institutions and Money, 54*, 177–189. https://doi.org/10.1016/j.intfin.2017.12.004

Baur, D. G., & Lucey, B. M. (2010). Is gold a hedge or a safe haven? An analysis of stocks, bonds and gold. *Financial Review, 45*, 217–229. https://doi.org/10.1111/j.1540-6288.2010.00244.x

Birkle, C., Pendlebury, D. A., Schnell, J., & Adams, J. (2020). Web of science as a data source for research on scientific and scholarly activity. *Quantitative Science Studies, 1*, 363–376. https://doi.org/10.1162/qss_a_00018

Boubaker, S., Goodell, J. W., Kumar, S., & Sureka, R. (2023). COVID-19 and finance scholarship: A systematic and bibliometric analysis. *International Review of Financial Analysis, 85*, 102458. https://doi.org/10.1016/j.irfa.2022.102458

Bouri, E., Das, M., Gupta, R., & Roubaud, D. (2018). Spillovers between bitcoin and other assets during bear and bull markets. *Applied Economics, 50*, 5935–5949. https://doi.org/10.1080/00036846.2018.1488075

Bouri, E., Molnár, P., Azzi, G., Roubaud, D., & Hagfors, L. I. (2017). On the hedge and safe haven properties of bitcoin: Is it really more than a diversifier? *Finance Research Letters, 20*, 192–198. https://doi.org/10.1016/j.frl.2016.09.025

Budler, M., Župič, I., & Trkman, P. (2021). The development of business model research: A bibliometric review. *Journal of Business Research, 135*, 480–495. https://doi.org/10.1016/j.jbusres.2021.06.045

Cheah, E.-T., & Fry, J. (2015). Speculative bubbles in bitcoin markets? An empirical investigation into the fundamental value of bitcoin. *Economics Letters, 130*, 32–36. https://doi.org/10.1016/j.econlet.2015.02.029

Chemkha, R., BenSaïda, A., Ghorbel, A., & Tayachi, T. (2021). Hedge and safe haven properties during COVID-19: Evidence from bitcoin and gold. *The Quarterly Review of Economics and Finance, 82*, 71–85. https://doi.org/10.1016/j.qref.2021.07.006

Chiaramonte, L., Dreassi, A., Piserà, S., & Khan, A. (2023). Mergers and acquisitions in the financial industry: A bibliometric review and future research directions. *Research in International Business and Finance, 64*, 101837. https://doi.org/10.1016/j.ribaf.2022.101837

Cobo, M. J., López-Herrera, A. G., Herrera-Viedma, E., & Herrera, F. (2011). An approach for detecting, quantifying, and visualizing the evolution of a research field: A practical application to the fuzzy sets theory field. *Journal of Informetrics, 5*, 146–166.

Corbet, S., Katsiampa, P., & Lau, C. K. M. (2020). Measuring quantile dependence and testing directional predictability between bitcoin, altcoins and traditional financial assets. *International Review of Financial Analysis, 71*, 101571. https://doi.org/10.1016/j.irfa.2020.101571

Corbet, S., Lucey, B., Urquhart, A., & Yarovaya, L. (2019). Cryptocurrencies as a financial asset: A systematic analysis. *International Review of Financial Analysis, 62*, 182–199. https://doi.org/10.1016/j.irfa.2018.09.003

Corbet, S., Meegan, A., Larkin, C., Lucey, B., & Yarovaya, L. (2018). Exploring the dynamic relationships between cryptocurrencies and other financial assets. *Economics Letters, 165*, 28–34. https://doi.org/10.1016/j.econlet.2018.01.004

Disli, M., Nagayev, R., Salim, K., Rizkiah, S. K., & Aysan, A. F. (2021). In search of safe haven assets during COVID-19 pandemic: An empirical analysis of different investor types. *Research in International Business and Finance, 58*, 101461. https://doi.org/10.1016/j.ribaf.2021.101461

Donthu, N., Kumar, S., Mukherjee, D., Pandey, N., & Lim, W. M. (2021). How to conduct a bibliometric analysis: An overview and guidelines. *Journal of Business Research, 133*, 285–296. https://doi.org/10.1016/j.jbusres.2021.04.070

Duan, K., Zhao, Y., Urquhart, A., & Huang, Y. (2023). Do clean and dirty cryptocurrencies connect with financial assets differently? The role of economic policy uncertainty. *Energy Economics, 127*, 107079. https://doi.org/10.1016/j.eneco.2023.107079

Dyhrberg, A. H. (2016). Bitcoin, gold and the dollar—A GARCH volatility analysis. *Finance Research Letters, 16*, 85–92. https://doi.org/10.1016/j.frl.2015.10.008

Elsayed, A. H., Gozgor, G., & Yarovaya, L. (2022). Volatility and return connectedness of cryptocurrency, gold, and uncertainty: Evidence from the cryptocurrency uncertainty indices. *Finance Research Letters, 47*, 102732. https://doi.org/10.1016/j.frl.2022.102732

Emich, K. J., Kumar, S., Lu, L., Norder, K., & Pandey, N. (2020). Mapping 50 years of small group research through SmallGroup research. *Small Group Research, 51*, 659–699.

Fry, J., & Cheah, E.-T. (2016). Negative bubbles and shocks in cryptocurrency markets. *International Review of Financial Analysis, 47*, 343–352. https://doi.org/10.1016/j.irfa.2016.02.008

Goodell, J. W., & Goutte, S. (2021). Diversifying equity with cryptocurrencies during COVID-19. *International Review of Financial Analysis, 76*, 101781. https://doi.org/10.1016/j.irfa.2021.101781

Gronwald, M. (2019). Is bitcoin a commodity? On price jumps, demand shocks, and certainty of supply. *Journal of International Money and Finance, 97*, 86–92. https://doi.org/10.1016/j.jimonfin.2019.06.006

Iqbal, N., Fareed, Z., Wan, G., & Shahzad, F. (2021). Asymmetric nexus between COVID-19 outbreak in the world and cryptocurrency market. *International Review of Financial Analysis, 73*, 101613. https://doi.org/10.1016/j.irfa.2020.101613

Jalal, R. N.-U.-D., Alon, I., & Paltrinieri, A. (2025). A bibliometric review of cryptocurrencies as a financial asset. *Technology Analysis & Strategic Management, 37*, 432–447. https://doi.org/10.1080/09537325.2021.1939001

Ji, Q., Bouri, E., Gupta, R., & Roubaud, D. (2018). Network causality structures among bitcoin and other financial assets: A directed acyclic graph approach. *The Quarterly Review of Economics and Finance, 70*, 203–213. https://doi.org/10.1016/j.qref.2018.05.016

Ji, Q., Bouri, E., Roubaud, D., & Kristoufek, L. (2019). Information interdependence among energy, cryptocurrency and major commodity markets. *Energy Economics, 81*, 1042–1055. https://doi.org/10.1016/j.eneco.2019.06.005

Ji, Q., Zhang, D., & Zhao, Y. (2020). Searching for safe-haven assets during the COVID-19 pandemic. *International Review of Financial Analysis, 71*, 101526. https://doi.org/10.1016/j.irfa.2020.101526

Kajtazi, A., & Moro, A. (2019). The role of bitcoin in well diversified portfolios: A comparative global study. *International Review of Financial Analysis, 61*, 143–157. https://doi.org/10.1016/j.irfa.2018.10.003

Kessler, M. M. (1963). Bibliographic coupling between scientific papers. *American Documentation, 14*, 10–25. https://doi.org/10.1002/asi.5090140103

Khan, A., Goodell, J. W., Hassan, M. K., & Paltrinieri, A. (2022). A bibliometric review of finance bibliometric papers. *Finance Research Letters, 47*, 102520. https://doi.org/10.1016/j.frl.2021.102520

Klarin, A. (2024). How to conduct a bibliometric content analysis: Guidelines and contributions of content co-occurrence or co-word literature reviews. *International Journal of Consumer Studies, 48*, e13031. https://doi.org/10.1111/ijcs.13031

Klein, T., Pham Thu, H., & Walther, T. (2018). Bitcoin is not the new gold—A comparison of volatility, correlation, and portfolio performance. *International Review of Financial Analysis, 59*, 105–116. https://doi.org/10.1016/j.irfa.2018.07.010

Korom, P. (2019). A bibliometric visualization of the economics and sociology of wealth inequality: A world apart? *Scientometrics, 118*, 849–868. https://doi.org/10.1007/s11192-018-03000-z

Kuo Chuen, D. L., Guo, L., & Wang, Y. (2017). Cryptocurrency: *A new investment opportunity? JAI, 20*, 16–40. https://doi.org/10.3905/jai.2018.20.3.016

Kyriazis, N. A. (2020). Is bitcoin similar to gold? An integrated overview of empirical findings. *Journal of Risk and Financial Management, 13*, 88. https://doi.org/10.3390/jrfm13050088

Lal, M., Kumar, R. B., Kumar, A., Saud, H. S., & Rai, V. K. (2022). Corporate social responsibility, accounting, and auditing: A retrospective review. *International Journal of Accounting, Business and Finance, 1*(2), 48–74. https://doi.org/10.55429/ijabf.v1i2.65

Liu, P., & Yuan, Y. (2024). Is bitcoin a hedge or safe-haven asset during the period of turmoil? Evidence from the currency, bond and stock markets. *International Review of Financial Analysis, 96*, 103663. https://doi.org/10.1016/j.irfa.2024.103663

Mensi, W., Sensoy, A., Aslan, A., & Kang, S. H. (2019). High-frequency asymmetric volatility connectedness between bitcoin and major precious metals markets. *The North American Journal of Economics and Finance, 50*, 101031. https://doi.org/10.1016/j.najef.2019.101031

Migliavacca, M., Patel, R., Paltrinieri, A., & Goodell, J. W. (2022). Mapping impact investing: A bibliometric analysis. *Journal of International Financial Markets, Institutions and Money, 81*, 101679. https://doi.org/10.1016/j.intfin.2022.101679

Mokni, K., Youssef, M., & Ajmi, A. N. (2022). COVID-19 pandemic and economic policy uncertainty: The first test on the hedging and safe haven properties of cryptocurrencies. *Research in International Business and Finance, 60*, 101573. https://doi.org/10.1016/j.ribaf.2021.101573

Mukherjee, D., Lim, W. M., Kumar, S., & Donthu, N. (2022). Guidelines for advancing theory and practice through bibliometric research. *Journal of Business Research, 148*, 101–115. https://doi.org/10.1016/j.jbusres.2022.04.042

Okorie, D. I., & Lin, B. (2020). Crude oil price and cryptocurrencies: Evidence of volatility connectedness and hedging strategy. *Energy Economics, 87*, 104703. https://doi.org/10.1016/j.eneco.2020.104703

Pandey, N., Andres, C., & Kumar, S. (2023). Mapping the corporate governance scholarship: Current state and future directions. *Corporate Governance: An International Review, 31*, 127–160. https://doi.org/10.1111/corg.12444

Patel, R., Migliavacca, M., & Oriani, M. E. (2022). Blockchain in banking and finance: A bibliometric review. *Research in International Business and Finance, 62*, 101718. https://doi.org/10.1016/j.ribaf.2022.101718

Paul, J., & Criado, A. R. (2020). The art of writing literature review: What do we know and what do we need to know? *International Business Review, 29*, 101717. https://doi.org/10.1016/j.ibusrev.2020.101717

Paul, J., Lim, W. M., O'Cass, A., Hao, A. W., & Bresciani, S. (2021). Scientific procedures and rationales for systematic literature reviews (SPAR-4-SLR). *International Journal of Consumer Studies, 45*, O1–O16. https://doi.org/10.1111/ijcs.12695

Platanakis, E., & Urquhart, A. (2020). Should investors include bitcoin in their portfolios? A portfolio theory approach. *The British Accounting Review, 52*, 100837. https://doi.org/10.1016/j.bar.2019.100837

Ramos-Rodríguez, A.-R., & Ruíz-Navarro, J. (2004). Changes in the intellectual structure of strategic management research: A bibliometric study of the strategic management journal, 1980–2000. *Strategic Management Journal, 25*, 981–1004. https://doi.org/10.1002/smj.397

Rubbaniy, G., Khalid, A. A., & Samitas, A. (2021). Are cryptos safe-haven assets during Covid-19? Evidence from wavelet coherence analysis. *Emerging Markets Finance and Trade, 57*, 1741–1756. https://doi.org/10.1080/1540496X.2021.1897004

Sandretto, D., Damilano, M., Goodell, J. W., & Paltrinieri, A. (2026). Multi-factor models of asset returns: A bibliometric analysis. *Journal of Economic Surveys, 40*, 739–760. https://doi.org/10.1111/joes.70039

Smales, L. A. (2019). Bitcoin as a safe haven: Is it even worth considering? *Finance Research Letters, 30*, 385–393. https://doi.org/10.1016/j.frl.2018.11.002

Somoza, L., & Didisheim, A. (2022). The end of the crypto-diversification myth. *SSRN Journal.* https://doi.org/10.2139/ssrn.4138159

Symitsi, E., & Chalvatzis, K. J. (2019). The economic value of bitcoin: A portfolio analysis of currencies, gold, oil and stocks. *Research in International Business and Finance, 48*, 97–110. https://doi.org/10.1016/j.ribaf.2018.12.001

Ugolini, A., Reboredo, J. C., & Mensi, W. (2023). Connectedness between DeFi, cryptocurrency, stock, and safe-haven assets. *Finance Research Letters, 53*, 103692. https://doi.org/10.1016/j.frl.2023.103692

Umar, Z., Gubareva, M., Teplova, T., & Tran, D. (2022). Covid-19 impact on NFTs and major asset classes interrelations: Insights from the wavelet coherence analysis. *Finance Research Letters.* https://doi.org/47102725-10.1016/j.frl.2022.102725

van Eck, N. J., & Waltman, L. (2010). Software survey: VOSviewer, a computer program for bibliometric mapping. *Scientometrics, 84*, 523–538. https://doi.org/10.1007/s11192-009-0146-3

Wang, P., Zhang, W., Li, X., & Shen, D. (2019). Is cryptocurrency a hedge or a safe haven for international indices? A comprehensive and dynamic perspective. *Finance Research Letters, 31*, 1–18. https://doi.org/10.1016/j.frl.2019.04.031

Wang, Y. (2022). Volatility spillovers across NFTs news attention and financial markets. *International Review of Financial Analysis, 83*, 102313. https://doi.org/10.1016/j.irfa.2022.102313

Wang, Z., Gao, X., & Gu, J. (2025). Can cryptocurrencies improve portfolio diversification? Evidence from the prospect risk perspective. *Research in International Business and Finance, 76*, 102828. https://doi.org/10.1016/j.ribaf.2025.102828

Weinberg, B. H. (1974). Bibliographic coupling: A review. *Information Storage and Retrieval, 10*, 189–196. https://doi.org/10.1016/0020-0271(74)90058-8

Yarovaya, L., Matkovskyy, R., & Jalan, A. (2022). The COVID-19 black swan crisis: Reaction and recovery of various financial markets. *Research in International Business and Finance, 59*, 101521. https://doi.org/10.1016/j.ribaf.2021.101521

Yousaf, I., Pham, L., & Goodell, J. W. (2023). The connectedness between meme tokens, meme stocks, and other asset classes: Evidence from a quantile connectedness approach. *Journal of International Financial Markets, Institutions and Money, 82*, 101694. https://doi.org/10.1016/j.intfin.2022.101694

Yousaf, I., & Yarovaya, L. (2022). Static and dynamic connectedness between NFTs, Defi and other assets: Portfolio implication. *Global Finance Journal, 53*, 100719. https://doi.org/10.1016/j.gfj.2022.100719

Zhu, S., Jin, W., & He, C. (2019). On evolutionary economic geography: A literature review using bibliometric analysis. *European Planning Studies, 27*, 639–660. https://doi.org/10.1080/09654313.2019.1568395

Chapter 4
Cryptocurrencies as a Financial Asset: An Empirical Analysis

4.1 Market Overview

Since the inception of Bitcoin in 2008, the universe of cryptocurrencies available to a prospective investor has expanded exponentially over the past decade and a half. One compelling reason for this expansion was certainly the popularity that Bitcoin gained in the early 2010s through media coverage as a new innovative, disruptive currency, and the establishment of the underlying blockchain technology, which inspired developers to create their own digital currencies. In tandem, the process of creating a new cryptocurrency was not as difficult as one might think, since the codes for cryptocurrencies were often open source and could be copied and replicated easily. Moreover, the creation of a new digital currency was relatively costless, hence, there were no disincentives to develop even cryptocurrencies with little meaningful functionality, aside from the time required to do so (Gandal & Halaburda, 2016). To give a numerical example of this universe, in Fig. 4.1, the evolution of the number of cryptocurrencies existing from August 2015 to December 2025 is reported.

The data refers to the number of digital currencies tracked by coinmarketcap.com, a leading source of crypto data in the literature (Griffin & Shams, 2020; Liu et al., 2022). As shown, between 2021 and 2025 the market experienced explosive growth, with millions of new cryptocurrencies emerging. By contrast, the period from 2015 to 2021 displayed a similar upward trend, but with a far less dramatic increase, amounting to only a few thousand coins, as highlighted in the zoomed section of the figure.

However, the aforementioned number of digital coins is only an approximation of the broader universe and should be interpreted as an upper bound of the investable cryptocurrency market, since it includes virtually any token created—even when the underlying project lacks credibility. Indeed, many of these coins fail shortly after their creation. In this regard, data reported by coingecko (2025)

D. Sandretto, *Cryptocurrencies as an Asset Class*, SpringerBriefs in Finance,
https://doi.org/10.1007/978-3-032-31491-8_4

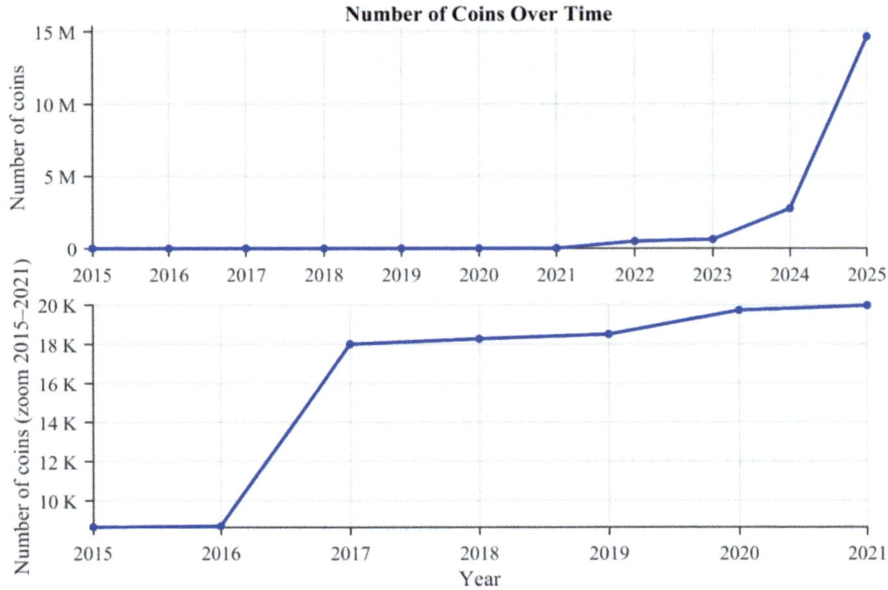

Fig. 4.1 Existing cryptocurrencies from August 2015 to December 2025. Source: Author's elaboration of coinmarketcap.com data using Matlab

documents that 53.2% of the cryptocurrencies tracked by its terminal since 2021 have failed, amounting to a copious number of over 13.4 million coins. The site also reports that the majority of these are low-quality effort meme-coin projects with the objective of using pump-and-dump strategies to scam investors. This raises the question: how could an investor mitigate the risk of allocating capital to such cryptocurrencies? One important, though not exhaustive, screening mechanism is to focus on cryptocurrencies listed on at least one exchange, since listing usually entails a minimal screening of the project's credibility. A reasonable proxy for coins with an observable traded price is the set of cryptocurrencies listed on coinmarketcap.com, which aggregates prices from multiple exchanges. As of December 2025, the number of tracked coins is around 9000, a very large figure but still far below the millions of tokens mentioned before. Even so, this still includes many small and illiquid cryptocurrencies that are unlikely to be suitable investments. For this reason, any investment should be preceded by careful due diligence on the project's white paper and a thorough understanding of the digital coin being considered.

Besides the sheer number of existing cryptocurrencies, an investor might be interested in another market dimension, namely their aggregated market value. Figure 4.2 depicts the overall cryptocurrency market capitalization using data from coingecko.com. As can be observed, the market capitalization has experienced several periods of growth and decline. Initially, it grew significantly during the period 2017–2018, marked by the explosion of Initial Coin Offerings (ICO), a system of capital raising through the issuance of tokens instead of traditional instruments

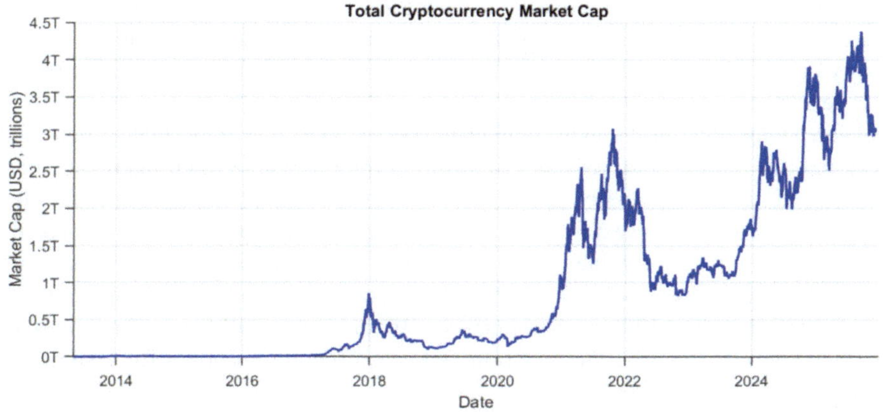

Fig. 4.2 Total cryptocurrency market cap from May 2013 to December 2025. Source: Author's elaboration of coingecko.com data using Matlab

(Howell et al., 2020). The ICO boom, however, subsided shortly thereafter, with market capitalization reverting to earlier levels until the onset of the Covid-19 pandemic. During this period, the market expanded dramatically, reaching a valuation of 2.5 trillion and then 3 trillion US dollars just before the end of 2021. This surge followed a phase of high liquidity due to expansionary monetary policies aimed at countering the economic crisis (Guo, 2024), as well as a process of institutionalization of cryptocurrencies, exemplified by Tesla's adoption of Bitcoin as a means of payment for its cars (Kovach, 2021). At the end of 2021, the market entered the so-called "crypto winter," during which market capitalization fell from the November 2021 peak of over 3 trillion to less than 1 trillion in June 2022, a 66% decline that persisted over time. This downturn has been attributed to a loss of confidence in the crypto sector following several high-profile scandals, such as the collapse and bankruptcy of the cryptocurrency exchange FTX, led by the founder Samuel Bankman-Fried, who was later found guilty of fraud related to the mismanagement of customer funds (Sherman et al., 2024). Another notable example is the collapse of the cryptocurrency LUNA in May 2022, linked to the failure of the algorithmic stablecoin TerraUSD, which had been the eighth-largest cryptocurrency by market capitalization, with nearly 40 billion US dollars in April 2022 (Lee et al., 2023). The arbitrage mechanism embedded in its smart-contract architecture—allowing the exchange of 1 UST (Terra) for 1 US dollar's worth of LUNA—proved unable to withstand the mass liquidation of UST. This triggered LUNA's collapse and led to a widespread loss of confidence among holders across the entire community (Liu et al., 2023). Furthermore, geopolitical tensions such as the Ukraine–Russia war and a tighter US monetary policy also contributed to the market downturn (Hermans et al., 2022). Investor interest reappeared in 2024 following the US Securities and Exchange Commission's approval of spot Bitcoin exchange-traded products in January 2024, as well as expectations of increasingly favorable regulatory regimes for crypto-assets under the new US administration led by Donald

Trump (Aerts et al., 2025). Finally, in 2025 the crypto market remained around an impressive valuation of 3 to 4 trillion dollars, partly affected by economic uncertainty due to tariffs imposed by the Trump administration and by unfulfilled promises regarding regulatory reforms.

Narrowing now the focus to market microstructure, it is important to note that although the market comprises thousands of cryptocurrencies, their aggregate market capitalization is actually quite concentrated in a small number of coins that dominate the overall investment segment. Notably, two main cryptocurrencies are considered the most prominent in the market: Bitcoin and Ethereum. As discussed in previous chapters, these digital currencies share strong visibility within the crypto community, but they differ in their purpose. Bitcoin is generally viewed as a cryptocurrency with a store-of-value function, whereas Ethereum is primarily designed as a smart-contract platform.

Of particular interest is Fig. 4.3, which shows that the combined weight of these two coins accounts for roughly 75% of total market capitalization, with troughs of approximately 50%. In 2014, Bitcoin was the dominant cryptocurrency, representing about 90% of total capitalization. In more recent years, however, this figure has stabilized at around 50%. Ethereum, by contrast, has consistently accounted for a smaller share—on average about 15% since its creation in 2015. The strong concentration in just a few assets has important implications for investors, since value-weighted crypto portfolios naturally become heavily exposed to Bitcoin's idiosyncratic characteristics. As will be discussed later in this chapter, this idiosyncratic component has so far played a positive role in shaping overall crypto market performance, but this may change in the future, as market maturation and the rise of alternative cryptoassets may reduce Bitcoin's relative dominance.

Lastly, the figure also highlights the growing importance of stablecoins, particularly in recent years, as a large number of users began adopting them for payment purposes, taking advantage of their price stability and store-of-value properties.

After examining the size of the cryptocurrency market and its principal actors, a final element to consider is the channels through which investors concentrate the vast majority of cryptocurrency trades: the exchanges.

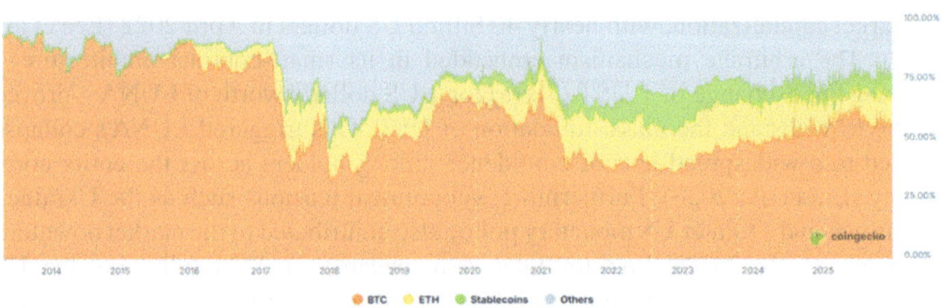

Fig. 4.3 Bitcoin and Ethereum market dominance from May 2013 to December 2025. Source: coingecko.com

In line with the evolution of the crypto market, the exchanges have likewise grown in number over the years and have established themselves as primary venues for the purchase and sale of cryptocurrencies. To outline this evolution, Fig. 4.4 shows the number of new exchanges created each year from 2018 to 2025, based on data from coinmarketcap.com. It stands out that the average number of new exchanges created per year is 122, with 2019 being the year with the fewest (19) and 2023 the year with the most (205). As of December 2025, coinmarketcap.com lists almost 250 centralized spot exchanges—led by Binance and Coinbase—and around 350 decentralized exchanges, with Uniswap and Pancakeswap being the most prominent. Despite the similar number of centralized and decentralized exchanges, the former still account for the majority of spot trading activity.

Alongside the high number of exchanges established, many eventually cease operations, reflecting dynamics similar to those observed in the broader cryptocurrency market. Several studies in the literature document cases of exchange failures and explain their determinants. For instance, Milunovich and Lee (2022) identify 238 cryptocurrency exchanges that existed between June 2010 and January 2021, and report that 45% of them did not survive over time. The main characteristics predicting default include poor security audits, low average trading volume, and limited operational history. Similarly, Sapkota (2025) surveys 845 unique crypto exchanges from 2010 to February 2023, of which 366, about 43%, defaulted. The author suggests that, beyond cybersecurity, age and transaction volume, centralized exchanges with high withdrawal fees and a limited number of listed cryptocurrencies are more likely to shut down. In light of this evidence, investors are advised to carefully select the exchange they use, since the choice of the platform can significantly affect the success of cryptocurrency investments (Levitin, 2022).

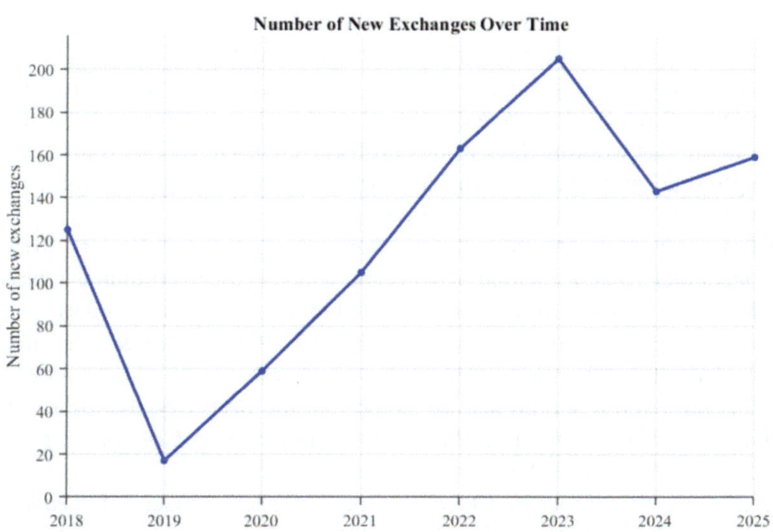

Fig. 4.4 Number of new exchanges over time. Source: Author's elaboration of coinmarketcap.com data using Matlab

4.2 Risk and Performance Features

The discussion now shifts to the risk and performance characteristics of the cryptocurrency market, which are of central relevance for investors. This section examines these aspects both at the level of individual assets, and in comparison with traditional asset classes. Particular emphasis is placed on Bitcoin, which represents the largest share of market capitalization within the crypto universe and is widely regarded as the flagship asset of the class. In addition, broader market proxies—constructed from indices that include a selection of high-capitalization cryptocurrencies—are considered to provide a more representative view of the asset class as a whole. The risk–return profiles of equities, bonds, commodities, and gold are also examined. Gold is analyzed separately, given its frequent comparison to Bitcoin as a store of value and its distinctive role within investment strategies (Harvey, 2025).

To conduct this analysis, data for the following Standard & Poor's indices were downloaded from the spglobal.com website, each corresponding to its respective asset class:

- S&P Bitcoin Index as a measure of Bitcoin
- S&P Cryptocurrency Top 10 Index as a measure of the core crypto market
- S&P Cryptocurrency Broad Digital Asset (BDA) Index as a measure of the broader crypto market
- S&P 500 Index as a measure of the equity market
- S&P U.S. Aggregate Bond Index as a measure of the bond market
- S&P GSCI Index as a measure of the commodity market
- S&P GSCI Gold Index as a measure of gold

The data were downloaded from the same site to ensure comparability across indices and consistency in their construction methodology. Furthermore, for convenience, the cryptocurrency indices were not manually constructed in order to avoid creating series that would not be aligned with traditional market indices, as the latter report data only on working days while cryptocurrencies trade 24/7, thus generating a non-negligible comparability issue. The S&P crypto indices take this into account and provide data conformed to the working week.

The timespan covered by the data goes from the beginning of January 2016 to the end of December 2025, for a total of 10 years, which is the maximum available data period from the aforementioned site. To enable a meaningful comparison across asset classes, the return time series are matched so that all indices share the same observation dates, while non-matched days are discarded. All indices are denominated in US dollars. It should also be noted that the S&P Cryptocurrency Top 10 Index has data available only from March 2018, and the S&P Cryptocurrency Broad Digital Asset Index from February 2017.

The data are then processed to obtain performance measures for each index. Specifically, daily returns are calculated as follows:

$$Return_{i,t} = \frac{PriceIndex_{i,t} - PriceIndex_{i,t-1}}{PriceIndex_{i,t-1}} \tag{4.1}$$

where *PriceIndex* is the price of index i at day t.

Subsequently, standard important measures are calculated for the returns to define the performance of each index. These measures are:

Arithmetic annual mean:

$$E(r_i)_{annual} = 252\, E(r_i)_{daily} \tag{4.2}$$

Annual Volatility:

$$\sigma_{i,annual} = \sqrt{252}\, \sigma_{i,daily} \tag{4.3}$$

Geometric daily mean:

$$E_g(r_i)_{daily} = \left(\prod_{t=1}^{N} (1 + r_{i,t})\right)^{\frac{1}{N}} - 1 \tag{4.4}$$

Arithmetic daily mean:

$$E(r_i)_{daily} = \left(\frac{1}{N}\right) \sum_{t=1}^{N} r_{i,t} \tag{4.5}$$

Daily volatility:

$$\sigma_{i,daily} = \sqrt{\frac{1}{N} \sum_{t=1}^{N} \left(r_{i,t} - E(r_i)_{daily}\right)^2} \tag{4.6}$$

Skewness:

$$Skew(r_i) = \frac{\frac{1}{N} \sum_{t=1}^{N} \left(r_{i,t} - E(r_i)_{daily}\right)^3}{\left(\sigma_{i,daily}\right)^3} \tag{4.7}$$

Kurtosis:

$$Kurt(r_i) = \frac{\frac{1}{N} \sum_{t=1}^{N} \left(r_{i,t} - E(r_i)_{daily}\right)^4}{\left(\sigma_{i,daily}\right)^4} \tag{4.8}$$

Daily Minimum:

$$r_{i,\min} = \min r_{i,t} \tag{4.9}$$

Daily Maximum:

$$r_{i,\max} = \max r_{i,t} \tag{4.10}$$

where N is the total number of return observations for the index considered and 252 is the conventional number of business days in a year, used to annualize measures.

4.2.1 *Cryptocurrency*

The first asset class analyzed is cryptocurrency. Three crypto indices are considered: S&P Bitcoin Index, S&P Cryptocurrency Top 10 Index and S&P Cryptocurrency Broad Digital Asset (BDA) Index.

As per the methodology outlined on spglobal.com, the S&P Bitcoin Index tracks Bitcoin with a price capture time of 4:00 PM ET. The index is calculated Monday through Friday, with no market holidays (S&P Global, 2025), and covers the period from the beginning of January 2016 to December 2025.

The S&P Cryptocurrency Broad Digital Asset (BDA) Index tracks the performance of digital assets listed on recognized open digital exchanges that meet minimum liquidity and market capitalization criteria covered by the S&P's data provider Lukka (https://lukka.tech/). This market value weighted index represents a broad investable universe, using the same price reference time and calculation days as the S&P Bitcoin index. It is rebalanced quarterly in March, June, September, and December. For inclusion, a cryptocurrency must meet the following criteria:

- Be exchanged on a data provider recognized exchange, eligible based on oversight, operational efficiency, data transparency, and data integrity
- Have traded for at least 3 months on that exchange and at least 60 calendar days during the 3 months prior to the rebalancing reference date
- Have a market capitalization greater than or equal to 100 million US dollars
- Have a 3-month median daily value traded (MDVT) of 100,000 US dollars
- Have a verifiable published white paper
- Not be a Stablecoin or a Privacy Token

All digital assets meeting these requirements are included in the index. As of December 2025, it comprises 229 coins and its available data runs from 28 February 2017 to December 2025.

Lastly, the S&P Cryptocurrency Top 10 Index is a market value weighted index tracking the top 10 cryptocurrencies by market capitalization. It is a subindex of the S&P BDA index, with the same price reference time and calculation methodology as the S&P Bitcoin index, and is rebalanced quarterly starting from March. Its data runs from 16 March 2018 to December 2025.

To illustrate the historical evolution of these indices, Fig. 4.5 reports their performance over time. Panels (a), (b), and (c) show the individual trajectories of each index using all available data, each normalized to a base value of 100. As can be seen and expected, all three follow the same dynamics as Fig. 4.2 in the previous section. Panel (d) shows the evolution of all three using the oldest common date across all indices, which is 19 March 2018. It can be observed that the three indices follow the same overall pattern, with the difference that the broader the inclusion of cryptocurrencies, the lower the resulting index performance.

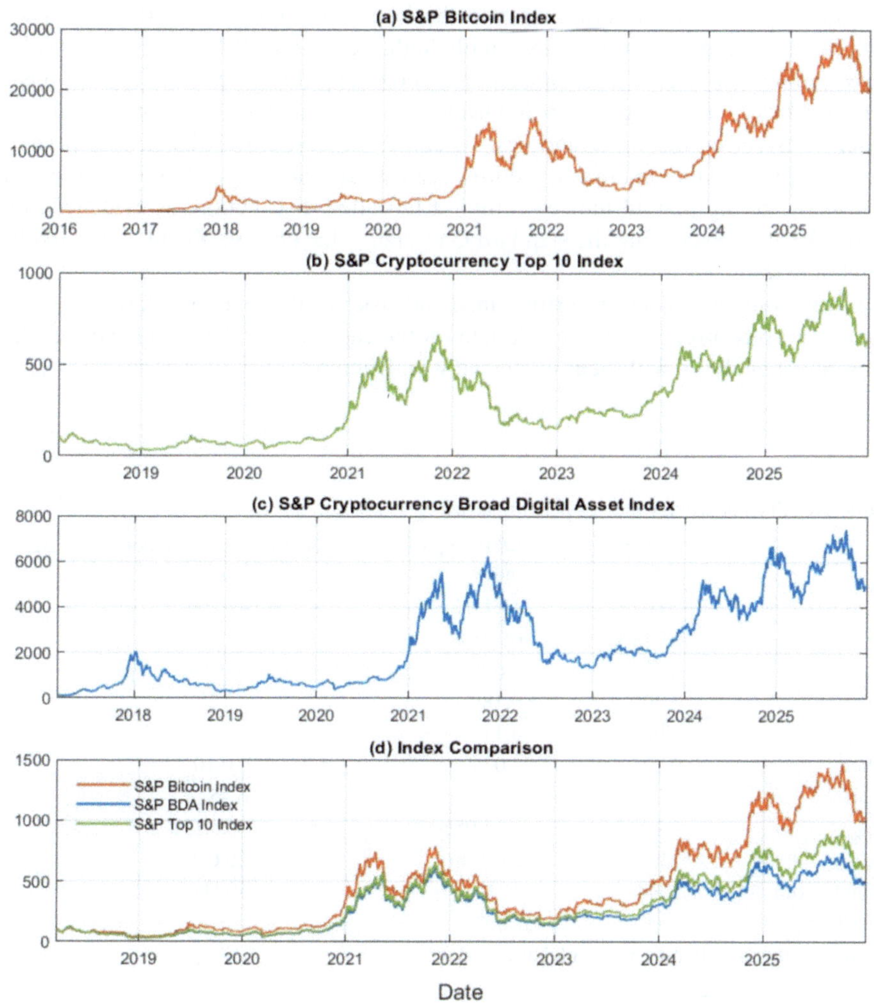

Fig. 4.5 Crypto indices evolution and comparison. Source: Author's elaboration of spglobal.com data using Matlab

Moving to performance measures, Table 4.1 reports these metrics for the three crypto indices. For a consistent comparison, all indices are evaluated starting from 19 March 2018.

It clearly stands out that Bitcoin alone has better performance compared to indices including a broader set of cryptocurrencies, with an annual average return of 50.07%. This result can be explained by the high correlation of other cryptocurrencies with Bitcoin combined with lower expected returns. In support of this, the correlation between the S&P Bitcoin Index and the S&P Cryptocurrency Top 10 Index is estimated to be 0.98, while the correlation with the S&P Cryptocurrency Broad Digital Asset (BDA) Index is 0.97. Of particular interest to investors are also the moments of the return distribution, which provide important information on the probabilities of future returns. Despite the impressive return performance of all indices, their annual volatility is extremely high, exceeding 60%, a level that may be excessive for risk-averse investors. Bitcoin shows slightly lower volatility but positive skewness, indicating lower downside risk compared to the broader indices. When considering the worst and best outcomes observed over the sample period, the minimum and maximum daily returns are very similar across all indices. Finally, it is worth noting that all indices exhibit a fat-tailed distribution, as evidenced by Kurtosis values exceeding the standard Gaussian value of 3, implying a high likelihood of extreme returns.

Given Bitcoin's superior performance and risk profile, and considering that the broader cryptocurrency indices lack data for the early part of the sample period, the subsequent analyses will focus exclusively on Bitcoin.[1]

Table 4.1 Cryptocurrency indices performance

	S&P bitcoin index	S&P cryptocurrency top 10 index	S&P cryptocurrency BDA index
$E(r_i)_{annual}$	50.07%	45.11%	42.26%
$\sigma_{i,\ annual}$	63.18%	65.21%	65.60%
$E_g(r_i)_{daily}$	0.12%	0.09%	0.08%
$E(r_i)_{daily}$	0.20%	0.18%	0.17%
$\sigma_{i,\ daily}$	3.98%	4.11%	4.13%
Skew	0.22	−0.04	−0.10
Kurt	7.76	6.63	6.45
$r_{i,\ min}$	−23.10%	−23.95%	−24.12%
$r_{i,\ max}$	23.47%	21.25%	20.61%
Number of observations	1944	1944	1944

Source: Author's elaboration of spglobal.com data

[1] Analyses using the other two indices, not reported in this chapter, do not qualitatively differ from the Bitcoin-only case, showing the same correlation coefficients with traditional asset classes and only a slightly lower risk-adjusted performance in the portfolio optimization analysis.

4.2.2 *Equity*

The equity asset class is represented by the well-known S&P 500 Index, widely used as a proxy for the US equity market, as it tracks 500 US large-cap companies and covers roughly 80% of total US market capitalization. The index is weighted using the float-adjusted market capitalization of each constituent and is rebalanced quarterly. Figure 4.6 illustrates the evolution of the index. Three major periods of market stress can be identified: the Covid-19 shock in 2020, the high-inflation environment and tighter monetary policy in 2022, and the tariff announcements made by the Trump administration in 2025, which triggered a market decline.

In contrast to the cryptocurrency indices, the S&P 500 series employed in this analysis is a total return index rather than a price index. Since cryptocurrencies do not distribute payoffs, the use of price indices was appropriate in that context. For equities, however, dividend payments must be incorporated. A total return index reinvests dividends into its valuation, and therefore the returns computed using Eq. (4.1) naturally reflect both price appreciation and the contribution of reinvested dividends. Using the same performance metrics as in the previous section, Table 4.2 reports the results of the analysis for the equity market over the period from the beginning of January 2016 to the end of December 2025.

As can be seen, the expected arithmetic return is lower compared to the previously assessed asset class, around 16% per year, but volatility is also way lower (18.18%). The remaining performance indicators also display more modest values relative to cryptocurrencies. The only metric exhibiting a higher figure is kurtosis, reflecting the fact that extreme events, when evaluated relative to a distribution with lower volatility, exert a larger statistical impact and become more concentrated in the tails.

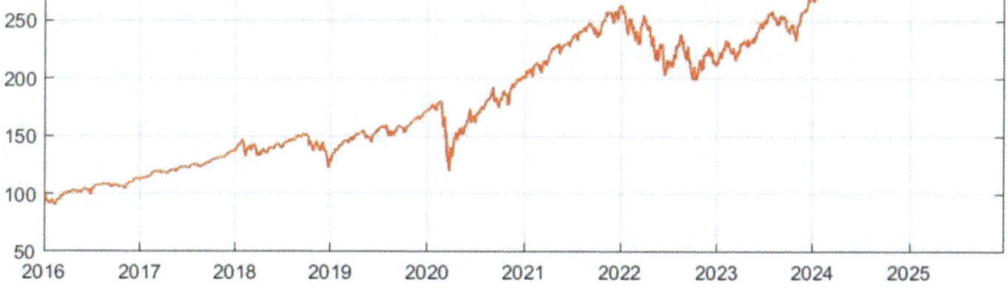

Fig. 4.6 S&P 500 Index evolution. Source: Author's elaboration of spglobal.com data using Matlab

Table 4.2 Equity index performance

	S&P 500 index
$E(r_i)_{annual}$	15.62%
$\sigma_{i,\ annual}$	18.18%
$E_g(r_i)_{daily}$	0.06%
$E(r_i)_{daily}$	0.06%
$\sigma_{i,\ daily}$	1.15%
Skew	−0.38
Kurt	18.60
$r_{i,\ min}$	−11.98%
$r_{i,\ max}$	9.52%
Observations	2496

Source: Author's elaboration of spglobal.com data

4.2.3 Bond

As a proxy for the bond market, the S&P U.S. Aggregate Bond Index is used for this analysis. This market-value-weighted index tracks the performance of the U.S. dollar-denominated investment-grade fixed income market, including U.S. Treasuries, quasi-government entities, supranationals, non-U.S. governments and agencies, corporates, covered bonds, residential mortgage pass-throughs, and taxable municipal bonds. Only bonds with fixed-rate, step-up, zero-coupon, and fixed-to-float coupon structures are eligible for inclusion. In addition, securities must be rated by at least one major rating agency (S&P, Moody's, or Fitch), be investment grade, and have a minimum remaining maturity of 1 month. Figure 4.7 depicts the evolution of the index. As with other asset classes, the bond market experienced notable stress during the Covid-19 shock in 2020, the high-inflation and tightening monetary policy environment in 2022, and the tariff announcements made by the Trump administration in 2025, which contributed to a market decline.

The index time series from January 2016 to December 2025 is calculated as a total return by aggregating the interest return, given by the return due to paid and accrued interest, and price return, which captures gains or losses due to end-of-day price changes and principal repayments. Table 4.3 provides the corresponding performance measures for the bond market.

As one might expect, the bond index average returns are lower than previous asset classes (2.17%), and volatility and other return distribution moments have relatively very low values. For instance, an investor holding the index would have experienced, at most, a daily gain of 1.63% and, at worst, a daily loss of 1.50% over the sample period. Importantly, the lower profitability of this asset class is explained by the fact that the index includes only investment-grade bonds and excludes high-yield (junk) bonds, which typically offer higher expected returns as compensation for their greater credit risk. By contrast, investment-grade bonds are characterized by a more conservative risk–return profile.

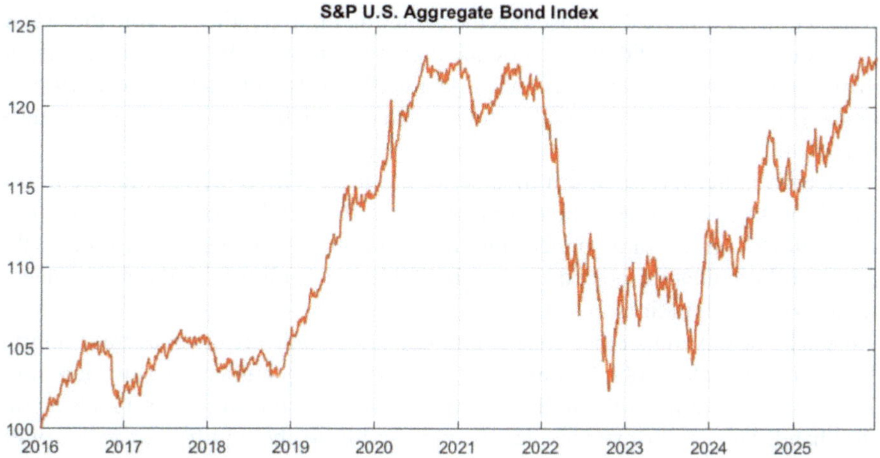

Fig. 4.7 S&P U.S. Aggregate Bond Index evolution. Source: Author's elaboration of spglobal.com data using Matlab

Table 4.3 Bond index performance

	S&P U.S. aggregate bond index
$E(r_i)_{annual}$	2.17%
$\sigma_{i,\ annual}$	4.22%
$E_g(r_i)_{daily}$	0.01%
$E(r_i)_{daily}$	0.01%
$\sigma_{i,\ daily}$	0.27%
Skew	−0.11
Kurt	6.13
$r_{i,\ min}$	−1.50%
$r_{i,\ max}$	1.63%
Observations	2496

Source: Author's elaboration of spglobal.com data

4.2.4 Commodity

Finally, the S&P GSCI Index is used to represent the commodity market, while the S&P GSCI Gold Index is considered specifically for gold. The former measures commodity market performance through futures contracts and is a production-weighted index designed to reflect the relative economic significance of each constituent commodity, while preserving tradability by restricting eligibility to contracts with sufficient liquidity. There is no limit to the number of commodities that may be included in the S&P GSCI. Nonetheless, eligible futures must reference a physical commodity, be denominated in USD, and be traded on an exchange operating in an OECD country.

The latter index, the S&P GSCI Gold Index, is a sub-index of the S&P GSCI and provides a reliable and publicly available benchmark tracking the COMEX gold futures contract. Figure 4.8 illustrates the evolution of both indices. From the graph, it is evident that gold did not experience major downturns like other asset classes, whereas the broader commodity index declined sharply during the Covid-19 pandemic. Furthermore, it is possible to note that gold began to rise significantly after 2024.

For both indices, total return time series are used. These incorporate the return from futures price changes, the roll yield arising from rolling expiring futures into new contracts on the same underlying, and the collateral yield, which reflects the return on the collateral posted as margin. Table 4.4 summarizes the performance measures for both indices.

It can be observed that the broad commodity index delivers lower average returns (8.37%) compared to gold, while exhibiting substantially higher volatility at around 22%, the highest among the traditional asset classes examined so far. Gold, on the other hand, shows performance levels comparable to the equity market but with lower higher-moment risk measures. Its kurtosis value, slightly below 7, indicates fewer extreme tail events relative to the broader commodity index, which displays a much heavier-tailed return distribution.

4.2.5 Risk Premium Comparison

After having assessed the performance measures for each asset class, it is now necessary to evaluate their risk-adjusted performance. In finance, returns alone are not sufficient to judge the desirability of an investment, because they must always be considered in relation to the risk borne by the investor. A common indicator used to compare different assets on a risk-adjusted basis is the Sharpe ratio (Sharpe, 1966), which measures how much excess return an investor receives for each unit of risk taken. The Sharpe ratio is defined as:

$$Sharpe\ ratio = \frac{E(r_i) - r_{risk\ free}}{\sigma_i} \tag{4.11}$$

where the numerator represents the annual average excess return of asset class i and the denominator represents the annual volatility of excess returns. Indices with higher Sharpe ratios are considered more efficient, in the sense that for the same level of risk, represented by volatility, a higher compensation is obtained. To compute the Sharpe ratio, it is necessary to determine the risk premium, which is the difference between the expected return of the asset and the return on a risk-free investment. The risk-free rate is retrieved from the 1-month Treasury Bill series available in Kenneth French's data library. A t-statistic for testing the hypothesis of a zero risk premium is also reported.

Importantly, as anticipated earlier, only the S&P Bitcoin index is considered among the cryptocurrency indices because it is the only one with a complete time

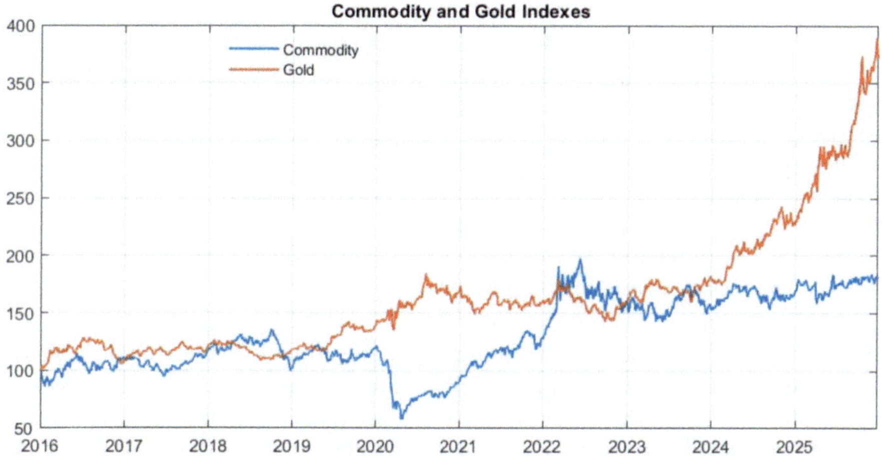

Fig. 4.8 S&P GSCI Index and S&P GSCI Gold evolution. Source: Author's elaboration of spglobal.com data using Matlab

Table 4.4 Commodity and Gold indices performance

	S&P GSCI index	S&P GSCI Gold index
$E(r_i)_{annual}$	8.37%	14.46%
$\sigma_{i,\ annual}$	21.92%	15.43%
$E_g(r_i)_{daily}$	0.02%	0.05%
$E(r_i)_{daily}$	0.03%	0.06%
$\sigma_{i,\ daily}$	1.38%	0.97%
Skew	−0.75	−0.17
Kurt	10.61	6.94
$r_{i,\ min}$	−11.77%	−5.73%
$r_{i,\ max}$	7.91%	5.76%
Observations	2496	2496

Source: Author's elaboration of spglobal.com data

series spanning the entire sample period. This makes possible an apples-to-apples comparison with traditional markets. Table 4.5 presents the resulting risk premiums, volatilities, t-statistics and Sharpe ratios for all asset classes.

Consistent with the earlier analysis, Bitcoin exhibits the highest excess expected return at 73.28%, statistically significant at the 1% level. It also displays the greatest volatility among all assets. Nevertheless, its Sharpe ratio of 1.11 exceeds that of every other index, indicating that investors were more highly compensated per unit of risk by holding Bitcoin during the sample period than by investing in any other asset.

Equity and gold show similar characteristics, with comparable risk premiums and volatilities. Bond and commodity, by contrast, deliver weaker risk-adjusted performance. The commodity index has benefited from quite remarkable returns in

Table 4.5 Risk-adjusted performance of indices

	S&P bitcoin index	S&P 500 index	S&P U.S. aggregate bond index	S&P GSCI index	S&P GSCI Gold index
Risk premium	73.28%	13.53%	0.08%	6.29%	12.37%
Std dev.	65.98%	18.18%	4.22%	21.92%	15.43%
t-stat	(3.50)	(2.34)	(0.06)	(0.91)	(2.52)
Sharpe ratio	1.11	0.74	0.02	0.29	0.80

Source: Author's elaboration of spglobal.com data

recent years, yet its volatility remains very high, resulting in a relatively low Sharpe ratio. The bond market offers only a negligible premium, reflecting the conservative nature of investment-grade securities. Its risk premium is indeed very close to the risk-free rate, making it the least attractive asset class in terms of excess return.

Overall, the data show that the most mean-variance efficient asset class over the past 10 years was Bitcoin, but the extent to which an investor would have borne the volatility is exorbitant. Moreover, it is important to note that this evidence does not imply that an investor should allocate the entire portfolio to Bitcoin. While the Sharpe ratio is a useful indicator for investment decisions, it does not account for the correlation among different investment opportunities. As Sharpe (1994) noted, an asset with a smaller Sharpe ratio may still improve the overall efficiency of a portfolio if it exhibits sufficiently low correlation with other holdings.

For this reason, the next section presents a correlation analysis and a portfolio optimization exercise in order to assess the potential diversification benefits of cryptocurrencies and to identify an appropriate allocation of this new asset class within a well-diversified and efficient portfolio.

4.3 Portfolio Overview

4.3.1 Correlations

One of the fundamental presumptions of portfolio diversification is that assets or asset classes should exhibit low correlation. The intuition is that in periods where one asset class performs poorly because of an idiosyncratic shock, others can perform fairly well, offsetting the negative outcome. The main provocation of Markowitz (1952) was that adding to an investor's portfolio an asset even with zero returns but with low correlation is attractive in the mean-variance framework because it may reduce variance and improve the risk-return trade-off by shifting the efficient frontier. In this sense, finding large negative correlations would be ideal, although observing such relationships across assets is not easy and, in particular, does not hold in the long term (Andersson et al., 2008; Molenaar et al., 2024; Strauss

& Williams, 2025). In light of this, the correlations among the asset classes under analysis are computed.

Correlations between index i and index j are calculated using the following formula:

$$\rho_{i,j} = \frac{\frac{1}{N}\sum_{t=1}^{N}\left(r_{i,t} - E(r_i)\right)\left(r_{j,t} - E(r_j)\right)}{\sqrt{\frac{1}{N}\sum_{t=1}^{N}\left(r_{i,t} - E(r_i)\right)^2}\sqrt{\frac{1}{N}\sum_{t=1}^{N}\left(r_{j,t} - E(r_j)\right)^2}} \tag{4.12}$$

As can be seen in Table 4.6, the correlation between Bitcoin and the other asset classes is quite low, ranging from 0.22 for equity to 0.02 for bond. Strikingly, an almost zero correlation is observed between the equity and bond asset classes, while gold has an estimated correlation with the bond index of 0.29. Additionally, the commodity index is positively correlated, although not strongly, with gold, reflecting the fact that commodities individually are subject to heterogeneous dynamics, in line with Fabozzi et al. (2012). It also has a negative correlation coefficient with bond and a positive value of 0.30 with equity. Interestingly, gold has a very low correlation with equity, equal to 0.04, although statistically significant.

But why are correlations low? This is partly inherent in the definition of asset classes, which groups assets that share common risk exposures driven by systemic factors specific to that category. In this sense, Bitcoin's very low correlation with traditional asset classes reflects the fact that its price dynamics are largely idiosyncratic, shaped by factors such as investor sentiment, adoption trends, hacking risks, and regulatory developments.

As widely recognized in the empirical finance literature, correlations are not static and can vary over time, especially in different market regimes (Strauss & Williams, 2025). In this regard, Babiak and Bianchi (2025) reported an increase in the co-movement between cryptocurrencies and traditional asset returns in the post-pandemic period. To assess whether similar dynamics emerge within our sample, Fig. 4.9 presents a 90-days rolling-window analysis of the correlations between Bitcoin and the other indices. This framework allows us to observe how these relationships evolve over time, with particular attention to periods characterized by market downturns.

Table 4.6 Correlation matrix across the indices

	Bitcoin	Equity	Bond	Commodity	Gold
Bitcoin	1.00				
Equity	0.22***	1.00			
Bond	0.02	−0.04**	1.00		
Commodity	0.09***	0.30***	−0.11***	1.00	
Gold	0.09***	0.04*	0.29***	0.18***	1.00

Source: Author's elaboration of spglobal.com data

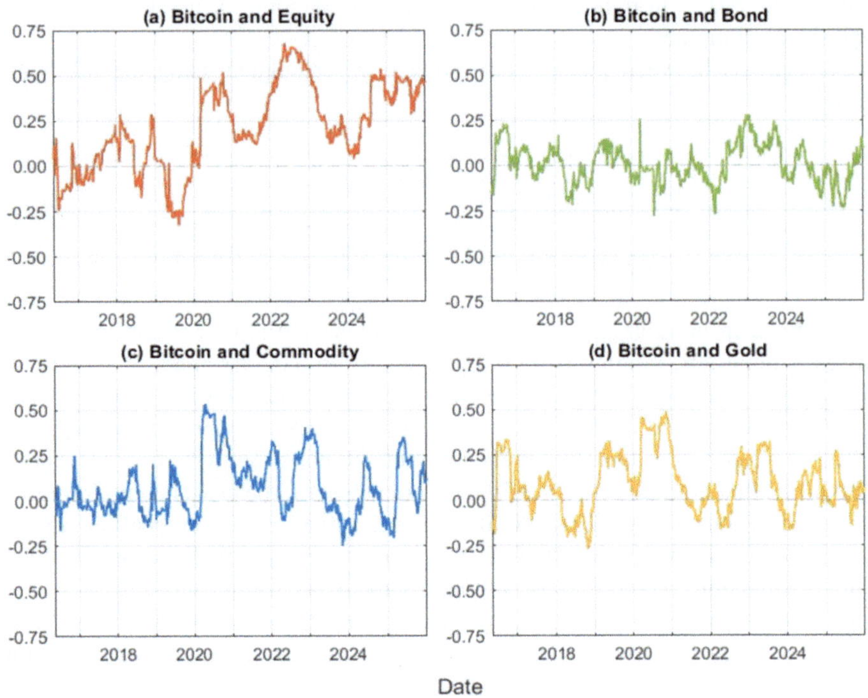

Fig. 4.9 90-days rolling window correlations between Bitcoin and other asset classes. Source: Author's elaboration of spglobal.com data using Matlab

From the figure, it is possible to notice that the values of the correlation coefficients vary greatly over time and especially in periods of bull or bear markets. Until the pandemic period in 2020, the correlation between Bitcoin and equity oscillated between a narrow band of −0.25 to 0.25, suggesting good potential diversification properties. With the onset of the Covid-19 pandemic, however, the correlation between the two asset classes rose sharply and remained persistently positive through the end of 2025, reaching levels close to 0.77 during the 2022 crypto-winter episode. Thus, the evidence of Babiak and Bianchi (2025) is confirmed. In contrast, Bitcoin maintained a very low correlation with the bond index, with rare peaks exceeding 0.25 in both directions, indicating weak co-movement with this asset class. Finally, commodities and gold became more correlated with Bitcoin during the pandemic, but then the correlation converged to prior levels, generally ranging between −0.25 and 0.30. These correlation patterns challenge the opinion that Bitcoin shares similar properties with gold. As the results point out, gold is largely uncorrelated with Bitcoin, so different factors govern their return dynamics.

Overall, the asset classes present generally low correlation in normal market conditions, with sporadic spikes during important market events. Nevertheless, the low correlations can be used fruitfully in constructing better diversified and possibly more efficient portfolios.

4.3.2 *Portfolio Diversification*

In this section, an empirical assessment of the diversification effect of cryptocurrency is presented. To build an initial visual intuition of the benefits of asset diversification, Fig. 4.10 shows the in-sample efficient frontier with and without the inclusion of Bitcoin in a multi-asset portfolio. The comparison highlights a clear improvement of the entire frontier once Bitcoin is added, with Bitcoin lying at the top in terms of expected returns. The portfolio represented by the S&P 500 is found as the highest point on the efficient frontier that does not take Bitcoin into account, very close to gold. The bond index, by contrast, is located at the opposite end, well below the efficient frontier. The same holds for commodities, which fall far to the right, outside the region spanned by efficient portfolios.

In light of this preliminary evidence, a more numerical assessment is now provided to quantify the role of cryptocurrencies in portfolio construction. To this end, a simulation of four portfolio allocations—with and without Bitcoin—is reported. The benchmark portfolio (BP) chosen for comparison is a 54%/36%/10% allocation to stocks, bonds and commodities (split into 5% gold and 5% broad commodities), which, as shown by Levine et al. (2018), outperforms the traditional 60%–40% stock-bond mix over the long run. Three additional portfolios are then constructed with varying levels of exposure to Bitcoin:

- Conservative portfolio (CP): 1% Bitcoin, 99% benchmark
- Moderate portfolio (MP): 5% Bitcoin 95% benchmark

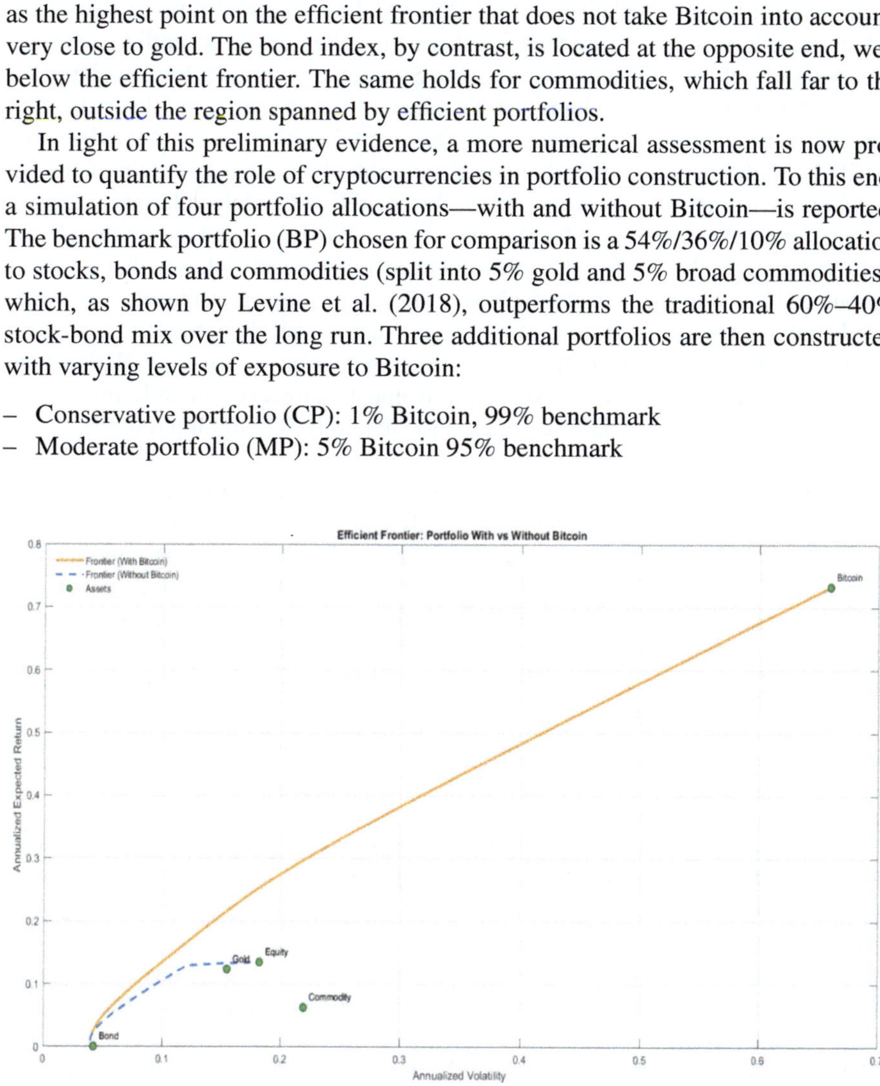

Fig. 4.10 Efficient frontier: Portfolio with and without Bitcoin. Source: Author's elaboration of spglobal.com data using Matlab

– Aggressive portfolio (AP): 10% Bitcoin, 90% benchmark

Each portfolio is rebalanced quarterly in order to have again the same initial asset class weights every 3 months. The portfolios run from January 2016 to December 2025, and excess returns over the risk-free rate are used to compute performance parameters. To account for the higher correlations observed after the Covid-19 period, a subsample analysis is also performed to capture this shift and its implications for asset allocation.

As shown in Table 4.7, the benchmark portfolio delivers average annual excess returns of 8.14% with volatility of 10.12%, yielding a Sharpe ratio of 0.80. This value exceeds those of most traditional asset classes analyzed earlier, with the exception of gold, which achieves the same Sharpe ratio but with lower volatility.

Introducing Bitcoin into the portfolio enhances performance and diversification benefits. Sharpe ratios rise progressively from 0.89 in CP to 1.28 in AP, driven primarily by higher returns rather than lower volatility. For instance, moving from BP to AP raises average annual excess returns by roughly 9%, while volatility increases by only about 3%. Moreover, the Sharpe ratio of AP is 1.28, greater than the Sharpe ratio of the single Bitcoin index, indicating once again the advantages of asset diversification. Interestingly, kurtosis declines as Bitcoin exposure increases, suggesting a reduction in the concentration of extreme returns, even though tail risk remains significant. This may reflect Bitcoin's periods of low or negative correlation with other assets, which help offset extreme movements. However, the minimum daily return worsens in AP (−7.53%) compared to BP (−6.05%), highlighting the persistence of downside risk.

More interesting evidence emerges when splitting the sample into the pre and post Covid-19 periods, where correlation dynamics appear to have changed for cryptocurrency and traditional markets (Babiak & Bianchi, 2025). A lower benefit from including Bitcoin is indeed observed in the post Covid-19 period, as its incremental contribution to the benchmark is around +6% in terms of annual returns and + 2.13% volatility, for a higher Sharpe ratio of 0.29. This is not as impressive as in the pre Covid-19 period, in which the contribution is +13.23% annual returns and + 4.89% annual volatility, for an incremental 0.74 Sharpe ratio. However, it is evident that adding Bitcoin to the portfolio provides a monotonic improvement in the Sharpe ratio from the benchmark portfolio to the aggressive one in both the pre and post pandemic periods.

Overall, it is possible to affirm that the inclusion of cryptocurrency in a portfolio improves risk-adjusted performance, and therefore investors can benefit from exposure to this asset, especially given that volatility does not increase excessively with a small allocation.

One question, however, remains partly unanswered, as this analysis only provided an example of the sensitivity of a small Bitcoin allocation within a naïve conventional portfolio.

What would have been the optimal allocation over the past decade to obtain the best mean-variance portfolio? Although this question might not seem particularly relevant for operational purposes, since this type of analysis cannot tell us much

Table 4.7 Performance portfolios

	Full sample				Pre Covid-19				Post Covid-19			
	BP	CP	MP	AP	BP	CP	MP	AP	BP	CP	MP	AP
$E(r_i)_{annual}$	8.14%	9.10%	12.80%	17.26%	6.17%	7.56%	12.98%	19.40%	9.55%	10.21%	12.70%	15.71%
$\sigma_{i, annual}$	10.12%	10.22%	11.25%	13.49%	7.83%	7.87%	9.35%	12.72%	11.50%	11.63%	12.44%	14.03%
Sharpe ratio	0.80	0.89	1.14	1.28	0.79	0.96	1.39	1.53	0.83	0.88	1.02	1.12
$E_g(r_i)_{daily}$	0.03%	0.03%	0.05%	0.06%	0.02%	0.03%	0.05%	0.07%	0.04%	0.04%	0.05%	0.06%
$E(r_i)_{daily}$	0.03%	0.04%	0.05%	0.07%	0.02%	0.03%	0.05%	0.08%	0.04%	0.04%	0.05%	0.06%
$\sigma_{i, daily}$	0.64%	0.64%	0.71%	0.85%	0.49%	0.50%	0.59%	0.80%	0.72%	0.73%	0.78%	0.88%
Skew	−0.6	−0.64	−0.66	−0.44	−1.14	−1.20	−0.79	−0.16	−0.46	−0.50	−0.60	−0.58
Kurt	15.58	15.6	13.43	11.35	13.24	13.57	11.02	11.53	14.07	13.98	12.91	11.10
$r_{i, min}$	−6.05%	−6.05%	−6.50%	−7.53%	−4.36%	−4.49%	−4.99%	−5.60%	−6.05%	−6.05%	−6.50%	−7.53%
$r_{i, max}$	5.04%	5.06%	5.15%	5.26%	2.54%	2.55%	2.60%	4.90%	5.04%	5.06%	5.15%	5.26%
Observations	2496	2496	2496	2496	1047	1047	1047	1047	1449	1449	1449	1449

Source: Author's elaboration of spglobal.com data

about the future, it is nonetheless interesting to understand what would have been the optimal allocation to span the realized efficient frontier over the past years, and the extent to which cryptocurrencies should have been included in the optimal portfolio. To address this, three optimized portfolios are calculated using the mean–variance framework. In line with the literature (Brauneis & Mestel, 2019; DeMiguel et al., 2009), the minimum-variance portfolio, the tangency portfolio, and the maximum-return portfolio are considered. These correspond to the lower and upper endpoints of the efficient frontier and the portfolio tangent to the capital market line implied by the risk-free rate. Methodologically, for each portfolio, the associated weights are obtained by solving the following optimization problems:

- Minimum-variance portfolio

$$\min_{w} w^T \Sigma w \tag{4.13}$$

$$\text{s.t.} w^T 1 = 1, w_i \geq 0$$

- Tangency portfolio

$$\max_{w} \frac{w^T E(r) - r_{risk\ free}}{\sqrt{w^T \Sigma w}} \tag{4.14}$$

$$\text{s.t.} w^T 1 = 1, w_i \geq 0.$$

- Maximum-return portfolio

$$\max_{w} w^T E(r) \tag{4.15}$$

$$\text{s.t.} w^T 1 = 1, w_i \geq 0$$

where w is the vector of indices weights, Σ is the variance covariance-matrix of indices returns, $E(r)$ is the vector of expected returns and $r_{risk\ free}$ is the risk free rate.

It is required that the portfolio is fully invested ($w^T 1 = 1$) and a short-selling constraint is imposed such that $w_i \geq 0$ for each asset i. Finally, the efficient portfolio returns are calculated by multiplying the vector of estimated efficient weights by the returns of the corresponding index. Weights are implicitly assumed to be held constant over time.

Table 4.8 reports the outcomes of the optimization analysis. Using the full sample from January 2016 to December 2025, the minimum-variance portfolio assigns the largest weight to the bond index, unsurprisingly given its low annual volatility of almost 4%. The maximum-return portfolio instead coincides with the Bitcoin index, which receives a weight of 100%, generating very high returns as seen before, but also very high volatility. By contrast, the combination of indices that composes the tangency portfolio is given by 50% gold, 30% equity and 20% Bitcoin, yielding

Table 4.8 Efficient frontier portfolios

	Full sample			Pre Covid-19			Post Covid-19		
	MVP	TP	MRP	MVP	TP	MRP	MVP	TP	MRP
$E(r_i)_{annual}$	0.90%	24.63%	73.28%	3.25%	13.13%	95.38%	0.03%	22.23%	57.30%
$\sigma_{i, annual}$	3.96%	17.61%	65.98%	2.39%	7.47%	73.34%	4.79%	17.07%	60.11%
Sharpe ratio	0.23	1.40	1.11	1.36	1.76	1.30	0.01	1.30	0.95
$E_g(r_i)_{daily}$	0.00%	0.09%	0.20%	0.01%	0.05%	0.27%	0.00%	0.08%	0.16%
$E(r_i)_{daily}$	0.00%	0.10%	0.29%	0.01%	0.05%	0.38%	0.00%	0.09%	0.23%
$\sigma_{i, daily}$	0.25%	1.11%	4.16%	0.15%	0.47%	4.62%	0.30%	1.08%	3.79%
Skew	−0.36	−0.12	0.26	−0.63	−0.15	0.32	−0.33	−0.27	0.15
Kurt	7.96	7.98	7.38	5.56	6.10	6.88	6.78	8.80	7.43
$r_{i, min}$	−1.92%	−8.97%	−23.11%	−0.90%	−2.75%	−21.39%	−2.03%	−8.30%	−23.11%
$r_{i, max}$	1.73%	7.07%	23.46%	0.53%	1.98%	23.46%	1.75%	6.62%	23.21%
Observations	2496	2496	2496	1047	1047	1047	1449	1449	1449
Weights									
S&P bitcoin index	0.00	0.20	1.00	0.00	0.08	1.00	<0.00	0.17	1.00
S&P 500 index	0.04	0.30	0.00	0.08	0.21	0.00	0.04	0.26	0.00
S&P U.S. aggregate bond index	0.92	<0.00	0.00	0.90	0.52	0.00	0.89	<0.00	0.00
S&P GSCI index	0.04	<0.00	0.00	0.02	<0.00	0.00	0.06	0.09	0.00
S&P GSCI gold index	0.00	0.50	0.00	0.00	0.19	0.00	0.01	0.48	0.00

Source: Author's elaboration of spglobal.com data

a Sharpe ratio of 1.40, with an average annual return of 24.63% and volatility of 17.61%. Despite the sizeable allocation to Bitcoin, the portfolio volatility remains lower than that of the equity market itself, once again highlighting the benefit of including this new asset class in a diversified portfolio. Analyzing the pre and post Covid-19 periods, different results emerge. For the pre Covid-19 period, the tangency portfolio is composed of 52% bond, 21% equity, 19% gold and 8% Bitcoin, generating a lower average return of 13.13% but also lower volatility of 7.47%, for an impressive Sharpe ratio of 1.76. The larger allocation to the bond index might be explained by its relatively higher returns in this sample, combined with low volatility and negative correlation with other assets. Indeed, the minimum-variance portfolio in this period shows an average return of 3.25% and is almost entirely composed of the bond index (90%). Bitcoin still dominates the maximum-return portfolio, with an average return of 95.38% but very high volatility of 73.34%, which may justify its lower weight in the tangency portfolio, as the additional risk brought by the digital asset may not be fully compensated by correlations with other assets.

In the post Covid-19 period, the minimum variance portfolio has a return slightly above zero and is again composed entirely of the bond index, which generates a null excess return in this period due to the strong impact of high inflation, which pushed its average return close to zero. The maximum-return portfolio is once again represented by a 100% allocation to the Bitcoin index, generating an excess return of 57.30% and volatility of 60.11%, lower than in the full sample. Finally, the tangency portfolio in the post Covid-19 period displays a risk-return profile very similar to the full-sample one, with a slightly lower Sharpe ratio of 1.30. This portfolio is composed of 48% gold, 9% commodities, 26% equity and 17% Bitcoin.

Despite changes in the correlation between Bitcoin and other assets, Bitcoin still plays an important role in multi-asset portfolio allocation in the post-pandemic era. In this regard, it is important to clarify that the higher optimal Bitcoin allocation in the second subsample, which may seem counterintuitive given the higher correlation with other assets, is an endogenous implication of the mean–variance solution, in which all weights are determined jointly as a function of the full vector of expected returns and the variance–covariance matrix. Hence, a regime shift in the volatility and correlation structure of non-crypto assets modifies the entire efficient frontier and, consequently, the marginal contribution of Bitcoin to portfolio diversification and risk-adjusted performance.

A final clarification concerns the fact that the analysis so far has focused exclusively on Bitcoin. Nevertheless, repeating the same analysis using broader cryptocurrency market indices yields qualitatively identical results. In particular, the optimal allocation amounts to approximately 12% when considering the S&P Cryptocurrency Top 10 Index and 10% when using the S&P Cryptocurrency Broad Digital Asset Index.

4.4 Conclusion

In conclusion, we have seen that the cryptocurrency market is highly fragmented in terms of the number of existing coins, but at the same time strongly concentrated in a small set of cryptocurrencies that drive overall market dynamics. Recent empirical evidence shows that cryptocurrencies—and Bitcoin in particular—have delivered the highest returns among the assets considered, while also exhibiting the highest volatility. This aspect makes the asset class potentially attractive, but one that requires caution and close monitoring.

The portfolio analysis highlights that adding an exposure to the crypto market can improve the efficiency of a multi-asset portfolio without making the overall allocation excessively risky. In the sample period considered, an allocation close to 20% to Bitcoin provided the best risk–return trade-off when combined with traditional assets. However, although this result might suggest allocating precisely that share of the portfolio to cryptocurrencies, it is important to acknowledge that this figure is estimated on historical data and should not be interpreted as a prescription for the future. In particular, estimation risk, extensively discussed in the literature (DeMiguel et al., 2009), raises doubts as to whether such an allocation would be optimal out of sample. The analysis also abstracts from market frictions such as transaction costs associated with rebalancing, which, while often limited in magnitude, may still affect the estimated performance. Moreover, analyses have been conducted considering a quite optimistic time period during which markets have experienced a strong growth. Given these considerations, a more conservative allocation in the range of 0% to 10%, depending on the investor's risk tolerance, is suggested. This range helps prevent cryptocurrencies from becoming an excessively dominant portfolio component in scenarios where the market experiences large drawdowns or pronounced swings that could destabilize the overall allocation performance, while still allowing investors to benefit from potential future growth of the digital asset segment.

References

Aerts, S., Born, A., Gati, Z., Kochanska, U., Lambert, C., Reinhold, E., & van der Kraaij, A. (2025). *Just another crypto boom? Mind the blind spots.* Financial Stability Review, European Central Bank, vol. 1.

Andersson, M., Krylova, E., & Vähämaa, S. (2008). Why does the correlation between stock and bond returns vary over time? *Applied Financial Economics, 18*, 139–151. https://doi.org/10.1080/09603100601057854

Babiak, M., & Bianchi, D. (2025). Mispricing and risk compensation in cryptocurrency returns. *Journal of Financial and Quantitative Analysis*, 1–27. https://doi.org/10.1017/S0022109025102329

Brauneis, A., & Mestel, R. (2019). Cryptocurrency-portfolios in a mean-variance framework. *Finance Research Letters, 28*, 259–264. https://doi.org/10.1016/j.frl.2018.05.008

Coingecko. (2025). *Dead coins: Over 50% of cryptocurrencies have failed*. https://www.coingecko.com/research/publications/how-many-cryptocurrencies-failed

DeMiguel, V., Garlappi, L., & Uppal, R. (2009). Optimal versus naive diversification: How inefficient is the 1/N portfolio strategy? *The Review of Financial Studies, 22*, 1915–1953.

Fabozzi, F. J., Füss, R., & Kaiser, D. G. (2012). *The handbook of commodity investing*. John Wiley & Sons.

Gandal, N., & Halaburda, H. (2016). Can we predict the winner in a market with network effects? *Competition in Cryptocurrency Market. Games, 7*, 16. https://doi.org/10.3390/g7030016

Griffin, J. M., & Shams, A. (2020). Is bitcoin really untethered? *The Journal of Finance, 75*, 1913–1964. https://doi.org/10.1111/jofi.12903

Guo, X. (2024). Exploring bitcoin dynamics against the backdrop of COVID-19: An investigation of major global events. *Financial Innovation, 10*, 58. https://doi.org/10.1186/s40854-023-00514-1

Harvey, C. R. (2025). *Gold and bitcoin*. https://doi.org/10.2139/ssrn.5530719

Hermans, L., Ianiro, A., Kochanska, U., Törmälehto, V.-M., van der Kraaij, A., & Simón, J. M. V. (2022). *Decrypting financial stability risks in crypto-asset markets*. Financial Stability Review, European Central Bank, vol. 1.

Howell, S. T., Niessner, M., & Yermack, D. (2020). Initial coin offerings: Financing growth with cryptocurrency token sales. *The Review of Financial Studies, 33*, 3925–3974. https://doi.org/10.1093/rfs/hhz131

Kovach, S. (2021). *Tesla buys $1.5 billion in bitcoin, plans to accept it as payment*. CNBC. https://www.cnbc.com/2021/02/08/tesla-buys-1point5-billion-in-bitcoin.html

Lee, S., Lee, J., & Lee, Y. (2023). Dissecting the Terra-LUNA crash: Evidence from the spillover effect and information flow. *Finance Research Letters, 53*, 103590. https://doi.org/10.1016/j.frl.2022.103590

Levine, A., Ooi, Y. H., Richardson, M., & Sasseville, C. (2018). Commodities for the Long run. *Financial Analysts Journal, 74*, 55–68. https://doi.org/10.2469/faj.v74.n2.4

Levitin, A. J. (2022). *Not your keys, not your coins: Unpriced credit risk in cryptocurrency*. https://doi.org/10.2139/ssrn.4107019

Liu, J., Makarov, I., & Schoar, A. (2023). *Anatomy of a run: The terra luna crash*. NBER Working Paper. https://www.nber.org/system/files/working_papers/w31160/w31160.pdf

Liu, Y., Tsyvinski, A., & Wu, X. (2022). Common risk factors in cryptocurrency. *The Journal of Finance, 77*, 1133–1177. https://doi.org/10.1111/jofi.13119

Markowitz, H. (1952). Portfolio selection. The. *Journal of Finance, 7*, 77–91. https://doi.org/10.2307/2975974

Milunovich, G., & Lee, S. A. (2022). Cryptocurrency exchanges: Predicting which markets will remain active. *Journal of Forecasting, 41*, 945–955. https://doi.org/10.1002/for.2846

Molenaar, R., Sénéchal, E., Swinkels, L., & Wang, Z. (2024). Empirical evidence on the stock–bond correlation. *Financial Analysts Journal, 80*, 17–36. https://doi.org/10.1080/0015198X.2024.2317333

S&P Global. (2025). *S&P digital assets indices methodology*. https://www.spglobal.com/spdji/en/documents/methodologies/methodology-sp-digital-assets-indices.pdf

Sapkota, N. (2025). The crypto collapse chronicles: Decoding cryptocurrency exchange defaults. *Journal of International Financial Markets, Institutions and Money, 99*, 102093. https://doi.org/10.1016/j.intfin.2024.102093

Sharpe, W. F. (1966). Mutual fund performance. *Journal of Business, 39*, 119–138. https://doi.org/10.1086/294846

Sharpe, W. F. (1994). The Sharpe ratio. *Journal of Portfolio Management, 21*(1), 49–58.

Sherman, N., Epstein, K., & Fleury, M. (2024). Fallen 'Crypto King' Sam Bankman-Fried gets 25 years for fraud. https://www.bbc.com/news/business-68677487

Strauss, J., & Williams, T. H. (2025). How to diversify differently: Time-varying correlations, determinants, and regimes. *The Journal of Portfolio Management, 51*, 64–82. https://doi.org/10.3905/jpm.2024.1.658

Conclusion

This book has provided a comprehensive examination of cryptocurrencies as a new and distinct asset class. The first chapter explored the complexity of how Bitcoin and cryptocurrencies in general function, along with the underlying DLT technology, which represents a core source of the value attributed to these assets. It further demonstrated how this value grows intrinsically as new innovations emerge, such as smart contracts on the blockchain. In this regard, Ethereum stands as the first mover and market leader, having enabled real-world applications for cryptocurrencies that extend well beyond their original role as a mere means of exchange.

The second chapter introduced a taxonomy and categorization of cryptocurrencies based on their functionality and infrastructure. A key takeaway for the reader is that cryptocurrencies are not all alike. Not all of them are comparable to Bitcoin, which was created primarily as a medium of exchange. Others are designed as tools to represent assets on-chain, run smart contracts, or provide access to goods and services. This is a fundamental point for any investor wishing to understand their different forms of intrinsic value.

Drawing on the academic literature, the third chapter confirmed that cryptocurrencies are regarded by scholars as a distinct asset class with meaningful portfolio diversification benefits, while also highlighting possible spillover effects and rising correlations with traditional assets during periods of market stress. Four main research streams were identified, covering the role of Bitcoin as a financial asset, spillover effects within and beyond crypto markets, the structural break caused by Covid-19, and the relationship between cryptocurrencies and commodity markets. In general, these findings offer useful implications for any reader seeking to integrate cryptocurrencies into portfolio construction strategies.

Finally, the fourth chapter presented an empirical analysis of the risk-return performance of several asset classes, including cryptocurrencies. For an investor, this chapter is essential for understanding that despite the extraordinary average returns delivered by cryptocurrencies, and Bitcoin in particular, over the past decade, the considerable volatility that comes with this investment must not be overlooked.

D. Sandretto, *Cryptocurrencies as an Asset Class*, SpringerBriefs in Finance,
https://doi.org/10.1007/978-3-032-31491-8

Importantly, when allocated in small proportions within a well-diversified portfolio, the benefits of inclusion are clearly positive, both before and after the Covid period, which brought an increase in the correlation between cryptocurrencies and traditional asset classes.

In conclusion, the message left by this manuscript is to approach cryptocurrencies with curiosity rather than fear, but also with great care and a thorough understanding of the subject, without which investors risk serious losses. Whether this phenomenon will continue to grow cannot be stated with certainty, but after nearly two decades of existence, cryptocurrencies have expanded significantly and are increasingly influencing the real economy. There are therefore good reasons to believe this trend will continue, and it will be the task of future research to further examine the evolving role of cryptocurrencies as a distinct and maturing asset class.

MIX
Papier aus verantwortungsvollen Quellen
Paper from responsible sources
FSC® C105338

If you have any concerns about our products,
you can contact us on
ProductSafety@springernature.com

In case Publisher is established outside the EU,
the EU authorized representative is:
Springer Nature Customer Service Center GmbH
Europaplatz 3, 69115 Heidelberg, Germany

Printed by Libri Plureos GmbH
in Hamburg, Germany